EDITORIAL

Liebe XING MAGAZIN *Leser,*

die Sommerausgabe ist da, und wie immer, skizzieren die besten Autorinnen und Autoren die wichtigsten Themen der Global Affairs.

FRANCOIS GODEMENT beginnt mit der ideologischen Ebene, der Soft Power, hinter der chinesischen Belt-and-Road-Strategie: *Xi Jinping's Rebranding of China's Messaging.* BERNHARD SEYRINGER fokussiert auf zwei "flag-ship"-Projekte der Belt-and-Road: das Hafenprojekt von Gwadar in Pakistan und der East Coast Railway Link in Malaysia.

STANISLAV SECRIERU vom European Institute for Security Studies hat ein interessantes Szeanrio für 2021 entwickelt: *What if ... Belarus and Kazakhstan quit the EEU?* Interessant weil beide Staaten Schlüsselfunktionen für den chinesisch-europäischen Eisenbahnverkehr haben, und sich Russland über die Eurasian Economic Union ein gehöriges Maß an Einfluß daran gesichert hat.

Russland ist auch das Stichwort im Essay von JAMES NIXEY vom Londoner Chatham House, der ein deutlicheres Aufzeigen von Regelverstößen seitens des Kreml fordert.

A World Wireless Network von HEIDI TWOREK erinnert uns daran, dass Information Warfare und der Zugang zu globaler Kommunikationsinfrastruktur nicht als neue Machtfragen des 21. Jahrhunderts aufgetaucht sind. Bereits im frühen 20. Jahrhundert wurde die gesamte Bandbreite an Political Warfare dazu aufgeboten: von der staatlichen Förderung neuer Technologien und damit verbundener Unternehmen, bis hin zu militärischen Interventionen.

DAVID ROWAN zeigt wie ein Software Gigant die Produktion völlig neu erfindet, und WOLFGANG LAMPRECHT erinnert uns an eine aktuelle Diskussion zur "Emergence of Corporate Citizenship".

Abschließend traf MORTEN GRONBORG, vom Copenhagen Institute of Future Studies, Erlend Hoyersten vom ARoS Art Museum in Aarhus, und sprach mit ihm über die Ausstellung Tomorrow Is The Question.

Viel Freude mit dem neuen Heft wünschen

   Ihre XING Magazin-Redaktion
   &
   Bernhard Seyringer, Herausgeber

PIERRE BONNARD
Die Farbe der Erinnerung

10.10.2019 – 12.1.2020

tresor im Kunstforum Wien
002-19

TAKE ON ME
ALFREDO BARSUGLIA
7.11.2019 – 12.1.2020

Kunstforum Wien

Freyung 8 | 1010 Wien | www.kunstforumwien.at | office@kunstforumwien.at | Tel.: +43 (0) 1 537 33 26

Pierre Bonnard, *Das Fenster*, 1925, *La Fenêtre*, Tate. Presented by Lord Ivor Spencer Churchill through the Contemporary Art Society 1930, N04494 © Tate, 2019 (Ausschnitt)
Alfredo Barsuglia, *Take on me*, Mixed Media, 2019 © Alfredo Barsuglia (Ausschnitt)

Partner des Bank Austria Kunstforum Wien

Medienpartner

Bildstrecke in diesem Heft: „University of Bristol - Historical Photographs of China"

1 Editorial
3 Inhalt / Impressum
4 Cartoon / Autoren
24 Die Redaktion empfiehlt …
   Neuerscheinungen am Büchermarkt.

François Godement 5
Xi Jinping's Rebranding of China's Messaging

INHALT

Bernhard Seyringer 12
Belt-and-Road:
Europäische und geopolitische Fragen.

James Nixey 21
Address Russian Rule-breaking.

Stanislav Secrieru 18
What if …
Belarus And Kazakhstan Quit The Eurasian Economic Union?.

Heidi J. S. Tworek 27
A World Wireless Network ::
German Ambitions by 1900.

David Rowan 29
Find your blind spots.
A software giant reimagines manufacturing

Wolfgang Lamprecht 31
The emergence of Corporate Citizenship

Morten Grønborg 38
Art, the Future, and the Dual Gaze

IMPRESSUM

XING–Magazin.
43, Jahrgang 16, 2019
ISSN 2075-2539

MRV Research, Wien
Herausgeber: Bernhard Seyringer
Einzelheft: 9,00 Euro + Versandkosten
Verkauf in ausgewählten Buchhandlungen und öffentlichen Institutionen,
Details unter **xing-magazin.at**

Redaktionsadresse: xing@curbs.at, XING c/o JKU-Inst. Päd./Psych., Altenberger Straße 69, 4040 Linz; Leserbriefe: office@xing-magazin.at;

Alle Rechte, auch die Übernahme von Beiträgen nach § 44 Abs. 1 und 2 Urheberrechtsgesetz, vorbehalten. Namentlich gekennzeichnete Beiträge geben nicht unbedingt die Meinung der Herausgeber wieder. Das Copyright sowie die Verantwortung für die publizierten Inhalte liegen ausschließlich bei den jeweiligen Autoren.

CARTOON

• •

AUTOREN

FRANCOIS GODEMENT ist Berater am Institut Montaigne in Paris und der Abteilung für Politische Planung im französischen Außenministerium; bis 2018 war er Direktor des European Council on Foreign Relations Asien& China-Programms;

MORTEN GRONBORG ist Chefredakteur von SCENARIO MAGAZINE, dem Magazin des Copenhagen Institute for Future Studies;

WOLFGANG LAMPRECHT ist Kommunikationswissenschaftler, Autor und Content Curator; einer der führenden Experten zum Thema Corporate Cultural Responsibility (CCR) in der Unternehmenskommunikation; Lehraufträge und Vorstandspositionen an mehreren Universitäten;

JAMES NIXEY leitet das Russland & Eurasien-Programm bei Chatham House;

DAVID ROWAN ist Publizist und einer der gefragtesten Redner zu Technologie & Innovation; war bis 2017 Chefredakteur von WIRED UK.

STANISLAV SECRIERU ist Senior Analyst am EUISS in Paris; davor war er am Polish Institute of International Affairs und am NATO Defence College in Rom.

BERNHARD SEYRINGER ist Politikanalyst, Gründer und Leiter von MRV Research und Herausgeber von XING Magazin für Politische Kultur;

HEIDI TWOREK ist Juniorprofessorin am Institut für Zeitgeschichte an der Universität von British Columbia, Gastprofessorin am Center for History & Economics der Universität Harvard und non-resident Fellow beim German Mashall Fund und am Canadian Institute for Global Affairs.

Xi Jinping's increasing grasp on power and its personalization coincide with far greater claims for China's influence and with a drive to assert China's interpretation of global values – or its own definition of these values. Yet before the Belt and Road theme started gaining international prominence, "win-win" was the most common theme from China in international relations, common enough to become the butt of jokes as to its interpretation, such as "China wins twice."

XI JINPING'S REBRANDING OF CHINA'S MESSAGING

TEXT: FRANÇOIS GODEMENT

Yet win-win is a child of free-trade rhetoric under the Clinton administration. What is uniquely Chinese is the ubiquitous use of the phrase in public diplomacy, and what is most telling is that China turned the table, using a Western-derived slogan to defend its status and interests within the world trading system.

Similarly, Xi has created or inherited keywords that are in themselves quite bland and certainly not unique. The "China dream" itself is of course borrowed from the American dream. "Creating a community of common destiny," as Hu Jintao was the first to express to China's neighbors, and "build[ing] a community of shared future for mankind," as Xi amplified in his January 2017 UN speech in Geneva,[1] are similar to Japanese mottos from an earlier era, such as *hakko ichiu* (eight corners under one roof), the slogan of the Co-prosperity Sphere. There is some recognition in China of this Asian linkage.[2]

Some will point out that the United States has claimed Manifest Destiny and that the EU seeks to attract partners on the basis of the values it upholds.[3] Xi is largely drawing from the repertoire of global values that is associated with post-1945 international institutions: Japan did so with the League of Nations in the 1920s. But he is also reclaiming the imperial legacy of the "great harmony under heaven" (*tianxia datong*) for BRI, claiming that the initiative will "stand on the international high ground of morality and justice"(*zhanjule guoji daoyi zhigaodian*).[4] In this regard, Xi hovers at the border of a more fundamental claim for Chinese values, echoing Yan Xuetong's praise for "humane authority" (*wangdao*), as opposed to hegemonism (*badao*), from the period of the Warring States on- »

Aus: Tellis, A. J.; Szalwinski, A.; Wills, M. (eds.). Strategic Asia 2019. China's Expanding Strategic Ambitions; NBA *The National Bureau of Asian Research, Seattle, 2019*; mit freundlicher Genehmigung des NBA;

1 Xi Jinping, "Work Together to Build a Community of Shared Future for Mankind" (speech at the UN Office, Geneva, January 18, 2017), http://www.xinhuanet.com/english/2017-01/19/c_135994707.htm.

2 See, for example, Feng Zhongping and Huang Jing, "China's Strategic Partnership Diplomacy: Engaging with a Changing World," European Strategic Partnerships Observatory, Working Paper, no. 8, June 2014, 17.

3 For a robust comparison with Manifest Destiny, see Yuen Foong Khong, "The American Tributary System," Chinese Journal of International Politics 6, no. 1 (2013): 1–47, https://doi.org/10.1093/cjip/pot002.

4 Han Zheng, "Xi Jinping: Tuidong gong jian 'Yidai Yilu' zou shen zou shi zaofu renmin" [Xi Jinping: Promoting the Common Construction of the "Belt and Road" for the Deep and Sincere Benefit of the People], August 27, 2018, http://cpc.people.com.cn/n1/2018/0827/c64094-30254137.html.

Banner outside the headquarters of "L'Association des Etudiants Chinois de Retour de FBS", Wuhan, 1938 © Historical Photographs of China

Legation guards outside city walls, Peking, 1905 © Billie Love Historical Collection / University of Bristol - Historical Photographs of China

ward.[5] This, however, happens within a speech aimed at Chinese audiences. The same ambiguity exists over the issue of a "Chinese model" for the economy, even if official pronouncements avoid the term. The concept's leading exponent, Fudan University's Zhang Weiwei, has recently produced a ten-part documentary titled "The Chinese Way" on the China Global Television Network (CGTN).[6] Liberal Chinese economists have denounced the temptation, insisting on China's integration with the global economy. Peking University's Zhang Weiying, for example, published two pieces in 2018 arguing that the notion of a Chinese model leads to conflict with the West.[7] This debate suggests tensions behind Xi's holistic approach.

Similarly, the theme of "common but differentiated responsibilities" has become a hallmark of China's stand on development and environmental issues. But it is far from original, having evolved from decades of international negotiation on natural resources and environment issues.[8] What matters is not the "Chineseness" »

[5] Yan Xuetong, "Chinese Values vs. Liberalism: What Ideology Will Shape the International Normative Order?" *Chinese Journal of International Politics* 11, no. 1 (2018): 1–22.

[6] Zhang Weiwei, "What Is the Unique Model Behind China's Rapid Rise?" China Global Television Network, March 26, 2018, https://news.cgtn.com/news/78497a4d7a6b7a6333566d54/share_p.html.

[7] Zhang Weiying, "Weilai shijie de geju, qujue yu Zhongguo zenme zuo" [The Future World Order Depends on How China Acts] (speech at the Symposium on Sino-U.S. Relations at the Institute of World Politics and Economics of the Chinese Academy of Social Sciences, Beijing, June 26, 2018), available in a version revised by the author at http://finance.qq.com/original/caijingzhiku/zhangweiying.html. A second article appearing on Peking University's website in October 2018 has been censored.

[8] For a genealogy of the terms, see "The Principle of Common but Differentiated Responsibilities: Origins and Scope," Centre for International Sustainable Development Law, Legal Brief, August 2002, http://cisdl.org/public/docs/news/brief_common.pdf.

> Beyond better competition and options for riders and drivers, the fact that individuals will be empowered by a broad 'transportation portfolio', a menu of options based on real-time information platforms, could ultimately enable a new mobility regime ...

or "un-Chineseness" of these concepts, but China's ability to project them, if only through ceaseless repetition and a drive to promote the concepts' language.

Often, the concepts are not only far from original but also vague or ambiguous. Xi's well-known Davos speech of January 2017 does cite or refer to four Chinese proverbs.[9] Yet it also refers to five foreign personalities, ranging from Charles Dickens to Christine Lagarde. The speech salutes multilateralism and multilateral institutions, certainly an opportune choice after the 2016 U.S. presidential election, and reads like an effort to mesh China's concerns with existing global values. Only in its conclusion does the speech land squarely on its feet, with a direct reminder in the first person of BRI and its international reception. At this point, we have left the domain of values to enter that of policy; we are also witnessing the rare case of a Chinese top leader directly promoting himself.

More than the content of the message, the repetition and the methods of influence or coercion – depending on the targeted audience – are what create its power. It is not that "Chinese can't think," including experts and diplomats, to borrow from the title of a famous book.[10] But in a system that combines Leninism and a high degree of personal power and personality cult, it is safer to repeat party lines. There is of course a similarity with the domestic sloganeering – what Simon Leys called the *langue de bois* (wooden language) inherited from Maoism. One can also surmise the unexpected influence of Confucianism with its insistence on zhengming (correcting names). The rectification of names, as this practice is also called, has often been seen as an empty ritual form. But modern language theory teaches us that language is indeed a form of reality – the person who controls the words controls far more. China does not want to direct behavior, it wants to condition it: "correct thinking will lead to correct behavior."[11] Xi has continued, after Hu, to encourage a form of civic Confucianism that was also practiced in Taiwan under Chiang Kai-shek and by South Korea's Park Chung-hee.[12] The latter's *yushin* (revitalizing) constitution is echoed by Xi's "national rejuvenation" (*minzu fuxing*) theme. In Xi's words, "don't forget your original sentiment" (*buwang chuxin*).[13] The spread all over the world of Confucius Institutes managed by an official Chinese state agency also attests to the quest for legitimacy from China's cultural heritage.

The drive for dominance through language applies to many domains of foreign relations. One need just go back to the promotion of the one-China principle, which is now accepted and enshrined in bilateral communiqués with nearly every nation (even if some manage to finesse the issue). The drive to create "strategic partnerships," some of them "all around" (Germany and Brazil), one described as "all weather" (Pakistan),

9 For the full text, see Xi Jinping (speech at World Economic Forum, Davos-Klosters, January 17, 2017), https://www.weforum.org/agenda/2017/01/full-text-of-xi-jinping-keynote-at-the-worldeconomic-forum.

10 Kishore Mahbubani, *Can Asians Think? Understanding the Divide between East and West* (Singapore: Times Books, 1998).

11 Bilahari Kausikan, "Manipulation, Chinese Style," *Nikkei Asian Review*, August 22, 2018, https://asia.nikkei.com/Opinion/Manipulation-Chinese-style.

12 Hamh Chaibong, "China's Future Is South Korea's Present," *Foreign Affairs*, September/October 2018, https://www.foreignaffairs.com/articles/asia/2018-08-13/chinas-future-south-koreas-present.

13 From Xi Jinping's report to the 19th CCP Congress, where expression is translated as "never forget why you started." The Chinese-language text is available at http://www.xinhuanet.com/english/download/Xi_Jinping's_report_at_19th_CPC_National_Congress.pdf.

Queen's Road Central, Hong Kong, 1924 © University of Bristol - Historical Photographs of China

and another as "comprehensive" (Russia), has become a charade with its bewildering variety of very similar terms.[14] The key term "comprehensive strategic partnership," often described as reserved for Russia, has also been used with regional groupings: first, the Association of Southeast Asian Nations (ASEAN) and second with the EU, which is a group of nations that have notorious divergences with the PRC on many major issues. Still, at times, it is the relationship with the United States that has been officially described as "the most important" relationship of all. More recently, regional agreements with the EU and ASEAN have also been framed with exactly the same language: three pillars of cooperation – political and security issues, economic and sustainable development, and social, cultural, and people-to-people exchanges.

The one-China principle is a key tenet for China, and it has been advanced worldwide. But this is »

14 This has almost been acknowledged as such by reliable PRC experts. See, for example, Feng and Huang, "China's Strategic Partnership Diplomacy," 18–19.

Banner slogan: "'We demand that the Japanese repay their blood debt!' The actual term used here for 'Japanese' is 'Dwarf pirates'. 1938 © Historical Photographs of China

Beyond better competition and options for riders and drivers, the fact that individuals will be empowered by a broad 'transportation portfolio', a menu of options based on real-time information platforms, could ultimately enable a new mobility regime …

now done through the language of interest, not that of values. One need only to look at the recent speech made by El Salvador's President Sanchez Ceren on the occasion of breaking ties with Taiwan and establishing diplomatic relations with the PRC: "This decision will allow for great benefits to the country and will bring extraordinary benefits to every one of us." [15] Foreign Minister Wang Yi salutes a decision to recognize one-China "without any precondition," but also holds out the prospect of tangible benefits for the country. There is nothing new, of course, in the money game played over the issue of recognizing or derecognizing Taiwan. What stands out today is that the game is out in the open, and in fact recognized as such by partner countries. The language chiefly used by China is that of pragmatism and self-interest, as these countries acknowledge. That perhaps trumps the value card.

The astonishing public success of the "One Belt, One Road" slogan with audiences all over the world also testifies to China's influence through public diplomacy. Partners have wanted to read so much into this grand design that it has had to be renamed an "initiative" for foreign consumption – emphasizing that there is no set strategy at work but rather a general offer of which others can avail themselves. Notwithstanding the huge number of conferences, think tanks, and academic institutions created in China around BRI, there has been more private skepticism about the initiative in China than abroad until recently. Like the Great Leap Forward – but with less ominous consequences, fortunately – BRI has met with a propaganda success that likely exceeds initial expectations. But this is not about "values," and perhaps not even about "policy," if one believes indeed the disclaimers from Beijing, which claims that the initiative has no set strategy. It is more about a promise of prosperity through massive projects and the money flowing around them.

China's promotion of values that it claims as its own, its de facto challenge to other values usually identified with a liberal international order, may be a part of its ascent toward the first rank of global powers – alone or *ex aequo* with the United States. But this could also be a marker of this ascent rather than a goal: what matters is less the values, or even the language, than compliance with China's interests and goals.

The contradiction between language and reality is a feature of advertising, which often chooses to hammer counterfactuals in order to hide weaknesses, as the tobacco industry has long practiced. Particularly striking is a recent CGTN advertisement displayed in airports and airline magazines. " 'See the difference' is our motto. CGTN is a practitioner of objective and balanced reporting," reads a caption next to the photo of a stylish young Karl Marx–type armed with an old-fashioned film camera. In a similar vein, at a Huawei event in Rome attended by three thousand people, the company, now barred from public procurement in the United States and Australia, pledged to provide "an open, innovative and collaborative digital ecosystem" for Europe. "Open" is another buzzword used by Xi. Both cases are good examples of the "virtual politics" used by post-Leninist authoritarian regimes to counter criticism.[16] Such slogans are propagated by modern mass media and can be used indifferently by public or semiprivate actors. «

15 This statement was made in an August 21, 2018, television address, as translated from Spanish. The original statement is available at http://www.presidencia.gob.sv/mensaje-a-la-nacion-del-senorpresidente-de-la-republica-salvador-sanchez-ceren.

16 See Andrew Wilson, *Virtual Politics: Faking Democracy in the Post-Soviet World* (New Haven: Yale University Press, 2005).

China hat mit dem 2. Belt-and-Road-Forum in Peking Ende April 2019 versucht, sich als verantwortungsvoller Akteur in der internationalen Arena zu positionieren. Deutlicher wurde allerdings, daß die finanziellen Mittel zur Umsetzung seiner globalen Ambitionen fehlen, westliche Investitionen dringend benötigt werden, und daß die Bedenken seitens der EU als bedeutungslos abgetan werden können.

BELT-AND-ROAD:
Europäische und geopolitische Fragen.

TEXT: BERNHARD SEYRINGER

Vierzig Jahre nach der beginnenden Öffnung Chinas blickt die Welt gebannt auf den beeindruckenden Aufstieg des Reichs der Mitte. Die chinesische Außenpolitik war seit den 1990er Jahren mit dem durch Deng Xiaoping geprägten Slogan "Hide your strengh, bide your time" umrissen. Mit der Belt-and-Road-Initiative haben die Nachfolger Dengs bereits 2013 eine Strategie für eine neue, chinesisch-dominierte Weltordnung vorgelegt. Mit einer dreieinhalb-stündigen Rede vor Kadern am 19. Kongreß der Kommunistischen Partei im Herbst 2017, hatte Xi Jinping zumindest das Gebot der Zurückhaltung über Bord geworfen.

Die internationale Diskussion zur chinesischen *Belt-and-Road-Initiative* (BRI) wird abwechselnd als Beleg für den unaufhaltsamen Aufstieg einer „asiatischen Zukunft", als überflüssige Zeitverschwendung, oder als strategisches Täuschungsmanöver beschrieben, um „Eurasien" mit den Mitteln der *„Schuldendiplomatie"* unter Kontrolle zu bringen. Schon vor der globalen Krise 2008/09 begann die chinesische Führung über außenpolitische Grundsatzfragen als auch, über das chinesische Entwicklungsmodell, mit der Betonung auf staatliche Investitionen und Exportorientierung nachzudenken. China wollte damit auch die nach dem Zweiten Weltkrieg entstandene Dominanz der USA in Asien, so weit wie möglich zurückdrängen. Aus chinesischer Sicht haben die USA einen C-förmigen „Containment"-Ring um China gelegt: von Japan, dem süd-chinesischen Meer über Indien bis Afghanistan. So gab es unter chinesischen und russischen Sicherheitsexperten Anfang der 2000er Jahre erhebliche Zweifel, ob die amerikanische Militärpräsenz in Afghanistan tatsächlich ausschließlich dem *„Krieg gegen den Terror"* galt.

Die chinesische Führung hatte mit Unterstützung einiger Intellektueller nach Ideen gesucht, die neuen chinesischen Ambitionen als kohärente Strategie neu zu formulieren. Der Armeegeneral Liu Yazhou sprach bereits 2001 *„vom notwendigen und schicksalshaften Marsch Richtung Westen"*, und Generalsekretär Jiang Zemin, skizzierte in einer Rede vor dem Nationalkongreß im Jahr 2002, eine zwanzig Jahre andauernde Periode an *„strategischen Möglichkeiten"*. Unterschiedliche Leitbegriffe, wie Zheng Bijian's *„Friedlicher Aufstieg"* vom November 2003, wurden abgelöst von „Friedlicher Entwicklung" und durch die catch-all-Phrase von der „Harmonischen Welt", formuliert von Präsident Hu im Jahr 2005, ersetzt. Wang Jisi hatte im Frühling 2011 in *Foreign Affairs* die Elemente einer chinesischen Suche nach »

Im Hintergrund arbeiteten chinesische Analysten an einer Neuinterpretation des konfuzianischen Hierarchiesystems, das ein kulturelles Wertesystem über Freiheit stellt, Ethik über Gesetz und Elitenführung über Demokratie und Menschenrechte.

der "Grand Strategy" formuliert. Viele Analysten in Peking betonen zwar, daß China nicht in die *Thukydides-Falle* tappen wird, nach der eine aufsteigende Macht die bestehende Weltordnung herausfordern wird, allerdings orten andere Stimmen sogar eine moralische Pflicht Chinas, genau diese Weltordnung und ihre Institutionen zu verändern, auch um die Interessen von Schwellenländern und der nichtwestlichen Welt besser zu vertreten.

Bei allen internen Diskussionen über eine chinesische *"Grand-Strategy"* war aber in der gesamten Regierungszeit von Präsident Hu (2002 – 2012) das Leitprinzip von Deng Xiaoping, die eigenen Fähigkeiten zu verbergen und den richtigen Zeitpunkt abzuwarten, beibehalten worden. Dessen Nachfolger, Xi Jinping, begann mit der neuen Ausrichtung, die "China-Story" zu erzählen. Wie Callahan darstellt, arbeiten im Hintergrund chinesische Analysten an einer Neuinterpretation des konfuzianischen Hierarchiesystems, das ein kulturelles Wertesystem über den Begriff der Freiheit stellt, Ethik über Gesetz und Elitenführung über Demokratie und Menschenrechte. Xi beschreibt bilaterale Beziehungen stets mit Begriffen wie „Freundschaft" (qin), „Aufrichtigkeit" (cheng), „beiderseitiger Nutzen" (hui) und „Inklusion"(rong). Alles dies sind Einzel-termini sowie modernisierte Rückgriffe auf konfuzianische Prinzipien.

1) DIE BRI: DER ELEFANT IM RAUM

Als offizielles Startdatum der BRI gelten zwei Reden Präsident Xi's im Herbst 2013: In der kasachischen Hauptstadt Astana, stellte er den *"Silk Road Economic Belt"* (SREB) und in Jakarta, Indonesien, die *"Maritime Silk Road"* (MSR) vor. Bei seiner Rede vor dem indonesischen Parlament verwendete Präsident Xi den Term *"Same Global Village"* und die Formulierung „*Schicksalsgemeinschaft*". Ersteres wird als ein Aufruf an regionale Nachbarn China's verstanden, letzteres ist ein Begriff, der seit 2007 Teil des offiziellen Vokabulars ist, ursprünglich um die Beziehungen zwischen Taiwan und der Volksrepublik zu beschreiben. Ein Bewußtsein für Public Diplomcay zeigt China auch darin, daß es Leitbegriffe stets überarbeitet und justiert hat: Aus der „*Neuen Seidenstraße*" wurde bereits 2014 *One-Belt-One-Road* und ab 2016 die *Belt-and-Road-Initiative*. Erwähnenswert ist, daß Präsident Xi nie von einer „*Neuen Seidenstraße*" gesprochen hat.

Es dauerte fast drei weitere Jahre bis China in einem detaillierteren Plan die bekannten sechs Korridore formulierte: 1) China-Mongolia-Russia Economic Corridor; 2) New-Eurasian-Landbridge Economic Corridor; 3) China-Central-Asia-West-Asia Economic Corridor mit zwei Routen; 4) Bangladesh-China-India-Myanmar Economic-Corridor; 5) China-Pakistan Economic Corridor; 6) China-Indochina-Peninsula Economic-Corridor. Das für eine derart ambitionierte Strategie adäquate Führungskomitee hatte sich im März 2015 unter dem Vorsitz des Vizepremiers und Mitglied des Ständigen Komitees des Politbüros, Zhang Gaoli (später ersetzt durch Han Zheng), gemeinsam mit Wang Huining, Chef der politischen Planung der Kommunistischen Partei, Wang Yang, Vizepremier und zuständig für den strategischen Dialog mit den USA in Wirtschaftsfragen, Yang Jiechi, Staatsrat für außenpolitische Fragen und Yang Jing, Generalsekretär des Staatsrates, konstituiert.

Es ist wenig verwunderlich, betrachtet man den zeitlichen Verlauf, daß die BRI als chi- »

Die USA fokussierten offiziell auf das Ziel der Integration und Stabilisierung Afghanistans nach dem Abzug der NATO Truppen. Es wurde aber für potentielle Partner schnell offenkundig, daß diese Absicht von der Obama-Administration bestenfalls halbherzig verfolgt wurde.

nesische Reaktion auf den amerikanischen "*Pivot to Asia*" und das Freihandelsabkommen TPP der Obama-Administration betrachtet wird. Die USA hatten den *Silk Road Strategy Acty* im Kongreß bereits 1997, 1998, 1999 und 2006 diskutiert. 2011 kam es durch die damalige US-Außenministerin Hillary Clinton mit der *New Silk Road Vision* zu einer Neuauflage. Mit ihrer Rede in Chennai in Indien am 20. Juli 2011 hatte sie den "*Pivot*" später umbenannt in "Rebalancing to Asia", offiziell formuliert und unter dem Titel *"Americas Pacific Century"* auch in *Foreign Policy* veröffentlicht.

Der damalige US-Verteidigungsminister, Leon Panetta, merkte im Juni 2012 explizit an, daß die USA beabsichtigen, 60 % ihrer Marinekräfte im indo-pazifischen Raum zu konzentrieren. Ergänzend dazu wurde eine engere Koordination mit den fünf wesentlichen Alliierten in der Region (Japan, Südkorea, Australien, Thailand, Philippinen) angestrebt, eine Vertiefung der Zusammenarbeit mit aufstrebenden regionalen Partnern (Indien, Indonesien und Vietnam), sowie eine Intensivierung der Kooperation mit multilateralen Organisationen wie ASEAN (Association of Southeast Asian Nations) und dem EAS (East Asian Summit) sowie der TPP (Trans-Pacific-Partnership).

Die USA fokussierten offiziell auf das Ziel der Integration und Stabilisierung Afghanistans nach dem Abzug der NATO Truppen. Es wurde aber für potentielle Partner schnell offenkundig, daß diese Absicht von der Obama-Administration bestenfalls halbherzig verfolgt wurde. Auffällig war, daß Präsident Obama selbst, die New Silk Road niemals ansprach, und daß für die Entwicklung regionaler Wirtschaftsbeziehungen, zwei der wichtigsten Nachbarn Afghanistans in der NSR fehlten: China und der Iran.

2) JÜNGSTE ENTWICKLUNGEN IM VERHÄLTNIS ZU EUROPA UND DER EU

Das im Jahr 2012 in Warschau gegründete 16 + 1[1]-Format hat sich im Rahmen der Konferenz im kroatischen Dubrovnik im April 2019 um das EU-Mitgliedsland Griechenland erweitert, und wurde zu 17 + 1. Wobei die Signale aus Athen durchaus ambivalent sind: einerseits, so meldet die griechische Tageszeitung Ekathimerini[2], wurde die weitere Entwicklung des Hafen von Piräus durch die chinesische COSCO untersagt, andererseits nähert sich die griechische Regierung China weiter an. Zweifellos ist auch der Beitritt Italiens, als erstem G7-Land, ein diplomatischer Erfolg für China.[3] Offiziell gilt Wirtschaftsminister Luigi Di Maio und seine 5-Sterne-Bewegung als die treibende Kraft, aber tatsächlich ist der Fädenzieher hinter den Kulissen Michele Geracci, ein enger Vertrauter von Matteo Salvini, der aber offiziell vor der „Kolonisierung Italiens" durch China warnt.[4]

»

[1] Anm.: das 16+1 Format wurde im Jahr 2012 gegründet: 11 EU-Mitgliedsstaaten (Bulgarien, Kroatien, Tschechische Republik, Estland, Ungarn, Lettland, Litauen, Polen, Rumänien, Slowakei und Slowenien) und 5 nicht-EU Mitgliedsstaaten (Albanien, Bosnien und Herzegowina, Mazedonien, Montenegro und Serbien)

[2] http://www.ekathimerini.com/239207/article/ekathimerini/business/athens-torpedoes-cosco-plans-in-piraeus

[3] "US Rebuke Sparks Rome Split on Chinese Investment Overtures", in Financial Times, 7 March 2019, p. 1, https://twitter.com/i/web/status/1103598699475881985.

[4] https://www.huffingtonpost.it/2019/03/11/salvini-frena-sulla-via-della-seta-dopo-il-si-tav-un-altro-passo-per-accreditarsi-a-bruxelles-e-washington_a_23689713/

China hatte im Jahr 2016 80 % seines Energiebedarfs aus dem Mittleren Osten und Westafrika über die Straße von Malakka importiert. Die daraus resultierende Verletzbarkeit Chinas macht die Bedeutung des Hafenprojektes im pakistanischen Gwadar deutlich.

Die Strategie der BRI-Mitgliedstaaten, die auch Mitglied der EU sind, ihre Nähe zu China als Druckmittel in Verhandlungen mit der EU zu nützen, scheint mittelfristig recht fragwürdig. Noch dazu, da sich bereits deutlich gezeigt hat, daß China in BRI-Staaten, wie etwa Polen oder Ungarn, keine wesentlichen Investitionen tätigt, sondern bestenfalls Kredite vergibt. Nur 12 % von Chinas Auslandsinvestitionen sind in BRI-Kooperationsländer geflossen,[5] oder wie es der Brookings Ökonom David Dollar formuliert: Ein BRI-Partnerland zu sein, bedeutet was Investitionen angeht, noch gar nichts.[6]

3) TAJIKISTAN: DIE ZWEITE MILITÄRBASIS AUSSERHALB CHINAS

China hat in Tajikistan eine zweite Militärbasis eröffnet. Es handelt sich dabei, nach Djibouti, um die zweite Basis außerhalb Chinas. Die Bereitschaft dazu motiviert China mit Bereitstellung von Krediten für Kraftwerke, Straßen und Pipeline-Projekten. In Tajikistan hat das chinesische Unternehmen TBEA ein 400 MW Kohlekraftwerk, Duschanbe 2, errichtet und im Gegenzug Schürfrechte bei unterschiedlichen Goldminen im Norden des Landes erhalten.[7] Es dürfte sich um die Überantwortung von landwirtschaftlichen Anbauflächen von mehreren tausend Hektar und ungefähr tausend Quadratkilometer Land, mit Gold und Uranvorkommen, nahe dem Wakhan-Korridor, an chinesische Eigentümer handeln.

Indien war bereits zwischen 2002 und 2010, im Rahmen seiner *„erweiterten Nachbarschaftspolitik"* in Tajikistan aktiv: Die erfolgte Instandsetzung des Flughafens Ayni (in der Nähe der Hauptstadt Duschanbe) erfolgte auch in der Hoffnung, Indien könnte MiG-29 Kampfflugzeuge und Kampfhubschrauber stationieren. Tajikistan hatte allerdings damals darauf bestanden, daß Russland einer solchen Stationierung zustimmen müßte, und blieb auch bei einer erneuten Anfrage 2015, bei diesem Prinzip. So ist die erfolgte Stationierung chinesischer Truppen ein deutliches Signal in Richtung Moskau.

4) PAKISTAN: GWADAR UND DER CHINA-PAKISTAN-ECONOMIC-CORRIDOR

Das *„Dilemma der Straße von Malakka"* wurde von Präsident Hu offiziell erstmals im Jahr 2003 angesprochen. Die Straße von Malakka ist ein relativ schmaler, 850 km langer Wasserweg zwischen der malayischen Halbinsel und der indonesischen Insel Sumatra. Sie ist zwischen maximal 15 km bis hin zu Engstellen von nur 2,5 km breit. China hatte im Jahr 2016 80 % seines Energiebedarfs aus dem Mittleren Osten und Westafrika über die Straße von Malakka importiert. Die daraus resultierende Verletzbarkeit Chinas macht die Bedeutung des Hafenprojektes im pakistanischen Gwadar deutlich: Im Falle einer Blockade durch amerikanische Marineverbände in der Straße von Malakka bietet Gwadar sicheren Zugang für China zum Arabischen Meer. »

---

[5] "Belt and Road Initiative Quarterly: Q1 2018," Economist Intelligence Unit, February 27, 2018

[6] David Dollar (2017) "Is China's Development Finance a Challenge to the International Order?" Japan Center for Economic Research Oktober, S.7

[7] "Risky Business: A Case Study of PRC Investment in Tajikistan and Kyrgyzstan." Jamestown, 18/14, 9.August, 2018

> Indien hat bereits deutlich gemacht, daß es gewillt ist zu militärischen Mitteln zu greifen, um seine geografischen Ansprüche (z. B. in Kaschmir) gegenüber China durchzusetzen.

Der China-Pakistan Economic Corridor (CPEC), einer der sechs Korridore der BRI, verbindet den Hafen von Gwadar in der pakistanischen Unruheprovinz Baluchistan mit Kashgar in der chinesischen Provinz Xinjiang. Der CPEC wurde erstmals beim Besuch des chinesischen Premiers Li in Islamabad im Mai 2013 erwähnt, wobei die pakistanische Regierung bereits im Februar 2013 die Leasing-Rechte an die staatlich-chinesische COPHC (China Oversea's Port Holding Company) vergab. Die Vereinbarung sieht vor, daß 91 % der Gewinne die Gwadar abwirft, von der COPHC beansprucht werden, 9 % die pakistanische Zentralregierung erhält, und keinen Anteil der Einnahmen für die lokale Regierung der Unruheprovinz Balutschistan. Mit dem Konsortium aus Singapur, das den Hafen von 2007 bis 2013 betrieben hatte, waren idente Bedingungen ausverhandelt.

Das pakistanische Militär betrachtet den CPEC als Gegengewicht und Verhandlungstrumpf in Verhandlungen mit den USA und gegen ein (aus pakistanischer Sicht) feindseliges Indien. Pakistanische Sicherheitskreise sind sich im Übrigen wohl bewußt, daß China möglicherweise weniger am Eisenbahnbau und der Hafenentwicklung interessiert ist, als Gwadar mittelfristig in eine Militärbasis zu transformieren. Das heißt allerdings auch, Pakistan wird die Vereinbarungen – auch unter den weithin unfair empfundenen Bedingungen – umsetzen.

Aus indischer Sicht sind der CPEC und der Hafen von Gwadar eine weitere Bedrohung indischer Sicherheitsinteressen durch China und dessen Verbündeten Pakistan. Es investiert daher, zusammen mit Russland und dem Iran, seit 2015 in den INSTC (India North-South Transport Corridor) dessen Verlauf vom iranischen Hafen Chabahar ausgeht. Chabahar liegt nur etwa 100 Meilen von Gwadar entfernt, und ist – neben dem Hafen von Dugm (Oman) als indischer Spiegel zum chinesischen Hafen in Djibouti – ein deutlicher Verweis auf die Absicht, Parallelstrukturen unter indischer Führung zu entwickeln. Indien hat auch bereits deutlich gemacht, daß es gewillt ist zu militärischen Mitteln zu greifen, um seine geografischen Ansprüche (zum Beispiel in Kaschmir) gegenüber China durchzusetzen.[8]

Wie kompliziert Bündnis-Entwicklung in der dortigen Region ist, läßt sich mit einem weiteren Akteur darstellen: Saudi-Arabien als traditioneller US-Verbündeter, wäre folglich auch an chinesischem Containment interessiert, und ein logischer Partner der indischen Initiative. Da der INSTC aber auch iranischen Interessen dient, ist Saudi-Arabien in einem mehrfachen Dilemma.

Für China ist der CPEC eines der wichtigsten geo-strategischen Projekte der BRI. Wo Djibouti dazu angelegt ist, den Suezkanal zu kontrollieren, ist Gwadar dazu in der Lage, den Zugang zum Persischen Golf zu kontrollieren.

5) MALAYSIA: DER EAST COAST RAILWAY LINK

Ein zweites geostrategisches Projekt, das im Rahmen der BRI vorangetrieben wird, ist der East Coast Railway Link (ECRL) in Malaysia. Im Rahmen des 2. Belt-and-Road-Forums Ende April 2019, gab der malayische Ministerpräsident bekannt, daß Malaysia nach längeren Neuverhandlungen und einem demonstrativen Ausstieg, das Projekt doch umsetzen wird.[9]

»

---

8 A. Ranjan (2014): The China–Pakistan Economic Corridor: India's Options. Delhi, Institute of Chinese Studies – Oc. Paper 10

9 "Malaysia is back on the BRI", The Asean Post, 20.April 2019, https://theaseanpost.com/article/malaysia-back-bri

Der jüngste pakistanische Terroranschlag in Indien (im Februar 2019) hat gezeigt, daß Pakistan islamische Terroristen im Land offen gewähren läßt, da es sich auf die diplomatische Hilfe Chinas – bis hin zum Veto im UN-Sicherheitsrat – fest verlassen kann.

Die Grundlage für den ECRL wurde im Rahmen des Peking-Besuches des malayischen Ministerpräsidenten Najib im November 2016 gelegt. Es handelt sich dabei um eine ca. 650 km lange Eisenbahnverbindung zwischen der West- und der Ostküste des Landes, die ebenfalls bei der Umgehung einer befürchteten Blockade in der Meeresenge von Malakka, für China äußerst nützlich wäre. Es soll damit der weniger entwickelte Osten des Landes (Pahang, Terengganu, Kelatan), mit dem besser entwickelten Westen verbunden werden. Konkret führt die Verbindung von Port Klang in der Region Selangor nach Kuantan Port auf der Ostseite. Die staatliche Export-Import Bank of China übernimmt die Finanzierung und der wesentliche Auftragnehmer und Projektentwickler ist die ebenfalls staatliche CCCC (China Communication Construction Company).

Der ECRL hat tatsächlich "game-changer"-Charakter für die Handelsroute durch die Straße von Malakka in Richtung Südchinesischem Meer. Es ist hier anzumerken, daß Containertransporte vom Seeweg nicht einfach auf Eisenbahntransporte verlagert werden können. Die kürzere Reisezeit von 135 Stunden (via ECRL) statt durch die Straße von Malakka via Singapur (165 Stunden) ist zwar eine Verkürzung um fast ein Fünftel, aber dennoch nur für hochwertige Güter möglich.

SIND DIE BRI-EISENBAHNPROJEKTE NUR EIN PROPAGANDA-INSTRUMENT?

Die Entwicklungen verdeutlichen unterschiedliche Befürchtungen: Erstens scheint es, als wären die Infrastrukturprojekte (mit Ausnahme der geostrategischen) zwar willkommen, letztlich aber nur von untergeordneter Bedeutung. Zweitens: Der jüngste pakistanische Terroranschlag in Indien (im Februar 2019) hat gezeigt, daß Pakistan islamische Terroristen im Land offen gewähren läßt, da es sich im Falle internationaler Isolation, auf die diplomatische Hilfe Chinas – bis hin zum Veto im UN-Sicherheitsrat – fest verlassen kann. Drittens: Peking hat klar gemacht, daß es das diplomatische Ziel – mit bilateralen Abkommen einen Keil zwischen die EU-Staaten zu treiben – recht günstig erreicht und nicht gewillt ist, auf geäußerte europäische Bedenken einzugehen.[10]

Die gelegentlich geäußerte Ansicht, die BRI wäre für Europa eine Chance to "re-enter the great game", ist mit Sicherheit zuviel an optimistischem Wohlwollen. Viertens: Das angeführte tajikische Beispiel zeigt, daß chinesische „Schulden-Diplomatie" auch von Staaten am Westbalkan ernst genommen werden sollte.[11] Der bekannte Fall des Hafens von Hambantota in Sri Lanka, gilt zwar als die *„Mutter aller chinesischen Schuldenfallen"*, ist aber keineswegs ein tragische Einzelfall, wie mancher Sinologe meint. Neueste Zahlen der New Yorker Rhodium Group zeigen, daß die Vorwürfe der „Schuldendiplomatie" keineswegs grundlos sind.[12]

Die im Rahmen des 2. BRF im April 2019 gezeigte *„neue Offenheit und Transparenz"* dürfte somit weniger ein Anzeichen für einen chinesischen Sinneswandel sein, als der Tatsache geschuldet, daß China nicht über die finanziellen Ressourcen für dieses Vorhaben verfügt. Es muß daher westliche Investoren daran beteiligen. Es wäre wohl zuviel an Ironie, wenn letztlich der Westen die chinesische BRI finanzieren würde, aus der Begründung heraus, daß man offenbar nicht dazu in der Lage ist, eigene Strategien zu entwickeln. Wie würde dieses Unvermögen mit einer etwaig-geplanten Militärbasis im Hafen von Piräus oder Triest umgehen? «

It was in November 2021 when the leader of the Russian opposition, Alexey Navalny, led street protests in Moscow against the rigged parliamentary elections which had taken place in late September. President Putin had not been seen in public for a month, and it was rumoured that he was being treated in a Swiss clinic ...

WHAT IF ...

Belarus And Kazakhstan Quit The Eurasian Economic Union?

TEXT: STANISLAV SECRIERU*

... Sensing the long-awaited arrival of post-Putin Russia, competition between elites flared up in Moscow: its first victim was the deputy finance minister, who was arrested on trumped-up charges of embezzlement of nearly $44 million. While domestic mass media speculated that the days of the prime minister were numbered, the power vacuum in the Kremlin, the inter-clan squabbles, and the revival of mass politics in Russia did not go unnoticed in the neighbourhood.

On 29 November, the presidents of Kazakhstan and Belarus emerged in Astana in front of TV cameras to issue short statements. "We set up the Eurasian Economic Union [EEU] six years ago with the hope that it would become a vehicle of comprehensive and mutually beneficial economic integration. Regretfully, despite our joint efforts to make it work, the EEU failed to deliver on the ambitious targets set and all of us are to blame for this", declared the president of Belarus. His recently-elected Kazakh counterpart followed: "In accordance with article 118 point 1 of the treaty,[1] this morning we notified the Eurasian Economic Commission about our decision to discontinue membership. Although we shall leave the EEU in 12 months, we will remain Russia's close military allies and therefore will respect all commitments undertaken within the Collective Security Treaty Organisation [CSTO]."

THE CONSEQUENCES

The announcement came as a bombshell for Russian governing elites, and provoked an intense debate about how to react. Young technocrats in the Russian government, who preponderantly saw the EEU as a liability and the idea of a common currency as dangerous for Russia's macro-economic stability, advocated for a swift and peaceful divorce. However, the prevailing outlook was one shared by the security elites: a double exit may trigger a domino effect among other members, and if the EEU disintegrates, the CSTO, the Russian-sponsored military alliance designed to maintain and augment Moscow's influence in the post-Soviet region, might follow suit. Given that any security and economic vacuum left would be filled by 'hostile powers', the reaction was to be firm so that no government would take post-Putin Russia lightly: disloyal EEU members were to be brought back to the fold, and the rest deterred from breaking rank. In the absence of the president, an informal meeting of the Russian security council quickly endorsed this approach. »

Reprint aus: Gaub F. (eds): "Scanning the horizon: 12 scenarios for 2021", Chaillot Paper / 150, 2019; mit freundlicher Genehmigung von EUISS - European Union Institute for Security Studies;

* The author would like to thank Marius Troost for collecting data for the diagram that features in this article.

Timeline

PRESENT (2019)
- Russia relies more on economic sticks than carrots
- Partners looking to diversify away from Russia
- EU's bilateral links with Minsk and Astana not fully exploited

SCENARIO (2021)
- Power vacuum in the Kremlin
- Street protests following Russian parliamentary elections
- Kazakhstan and Belarus leave EEU

CONSEQUENCES (2021+)
- Russia responds with economic and cyberwarfare
- EU tries to help but is struck by Russian cyber attacks
- Other members consider leaving the EEU

Military options were rapidly discarded, as Russia's military was visibly overstretched. Over the last two years, Moscow had sent more troops to Syria, deployed special forces to Libya, and beefed up its presence in Tajikistan to repel a potential Daesh offensive from Afghanistan (after the terrorist group expanded its foothold to the north of the country). Lacking the firepower and political will to launch another military adventure, Moscow decided to employ a combination of political and economic sabotage techniques, with a heavy reliance on cyber statecraft.

In line with this approach, documentaries were aired on Russian TV channels containing *kompromat* (compromising material) on the presidents of Belarus and Kazakhstan, import bans on food products were put in place due to alleged violations of phytosanitary standards, while the police conducted raids to expel hundreds of Kazakh and Belarusian citizens from Moscow. In parallel, the banking sector, airports, refineries, gas and oil pipelines and electricity distribution networks in Kazakhstan and Belarus were struck by a wave of cyberattacks. In response to calls for assistance from Minsk and Astana, several EU member states deployed Computer Emergency Readiness Teams (CERTs) to help deal with the repercussions of these cyber-assaults. Shortly after, Gazprom announced that North Stream 2 gas pipelines were to be temporarily closed for 'planned' maintenance works. At the same time, several EU member states experienced waves of cyberattacks against commercial banks, power grids and e-health infrastructure.

Russia's response had a number of intended and unintended strategic implications. First, when cyberattacks hit the Kazakh and Belarusian populations (and both governments attributed them to Moscow), Russia's popularity in both countries plummeted. Second, coercive measures took a heavy toll on local economies (energy resources made up 20 % of Belarus' and 75 % of Kazakhstan's exports), forcing both countries to speed up economic diversification. Third, instead of acting as a deterrent, Russia's heavy-handed approach prompted other members to consider leaving the EEU, too. Fourth, the disruption of oil and gas deliveries entrenched the image of Russia as an unreliable energy provider. Fifth, massive cyberattacks in Europe, and the related financial losses, eroded Europeans' trust in the digital economy and e-solutions. Last but not least, Russia's response made any attempts to put the EU-Russia relations on a new positive footing in the short and medium-term impossible.

HOW DID THIS HAPPEN?

The original sin of the EEU was that the Kremlin designed it more as a vehicle to institutionalise Russia's geopolitical pre-eminence in the post-Soviet region rather than to foster horizontal economic integration. For Moscow, regardless of the legal provision which allows for a state to exit the Union, once a country had joined the EEU there was no »

1 "The Treaty of Eurasian Economic Union," May 29, 2014 http://www.un.org/en/ga/sixth/70/docs/treaty_on_eeu.pdf.

turning back. This logic of geopolitical patrimonialism led Russia to retaliate in a way which inflicted losses on its own economy, precipitated the collapse of the EEU and deepened mistrust with its main trading partner – the EU.

Russia had focussed more on what it wanted and less on what its allies needed. With the economy stagnating, Moscow increasingly relied on ever-larger sticks and ever-smaller carrots to keep ranks closed, nurturing frustration among EEU member states. While Russia's direct and indirect support for Belarus amounted to 26 % of Gross Domestic Product (GDP) in 2006, in 2016 it stood at little over 5 % of GDP.2 And in 2017, Belarus's trade turnover with Russia amounted to $ 26 billion, some $ 2 billion less than in 2010.[3] Russia's trade with Kazakhstan had also been on a downward trajectory for some time, decreasing by 37 % between 2011 and 2016.[4] Despite these trends, Russia continued to develop and press ideas on how to deepen integration (the introduction of a common currency, for instance) without delivering on previous commitments (such as the elimination of non-tariff trade barriers). Unsurprisingly, EEU members pondered gradual economic diversification (for example, Belarusian President Lukashenko's proposed geographic formula 30-30-30, whereby the country's exports are divided equally between Russia, the EU and the rest of the world[5]) in order to avert what is seen in Astana and Minsk as a creeping attempt to swallow them economically, disguised as 'mutually beneficial' integration.

2 Ivan Tkachev and Anton Feinberg, "Skrytii schiot na 100 mlrd: kak Rossia soderjit belorusskuiu ekonomiku [Hidden account for 100 billion: How Russia sustains Belarus' economy]," RBK, April 2, 2017 https://www.rbc.ru/economics/02/04/2017/58e026879a79471d6c8aef30.

3 "Tovarooborot mejdu Rossiei i Belarusiu v 2017 godu dostig $26 mlrd [The Trade Turnover Between Russia and Belarus in 2017 Reached $26 Billion]," BelTa, December 26, 2017 http://www.belta.by/economics/view/tovarooborot-mezhdu-rossiej-ibelarusjju-v-2017-godu-dostig-26-mlrd-282082-2017/.

4 Roman Mamchitz, "Pochemu sokratilasi torgovlia mejdu Rossiei i Kazakhstanom? [Why did Trade Between Russia and Kazakhstan Decrease?]," Invest-Forsight, November 24, 2017 https://www.if24.ru/torgovlya-rossia-kazakhstan/.

5 "Belarus Invites Belgium to Partake in Great Stone Projects", BelTa, March 3, 2016 http://eng.belta.by/economics/view/belarusinvites-belgium-to-partake-in-great-stone-projects-89344-2016/.

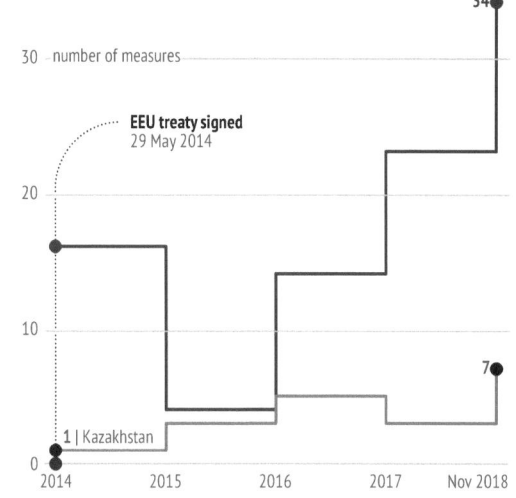

Increase in Russian economic restrictions against allies Measures that have impeded trade, transportation or energy supply, 2014 - November 2018

Data: 365info.kz, 2016; Fsvps.ru, 2018; GordonUA.com, 2018; Informburo.kz, 2017; Kommersant.ru, 2014–2018; NG.ru, 2014 & 2016

The EU, for its part, would have been better positioned to soften the impact of Russia's coercive measures against Belarus and Kazakhstan if trade relations and infrastructure connections had been deeper with each respective country, and if emerging digital economy sectors had been better protected against malicious cyber intrusions. EU-Belarus relations, for instance, were still governed by the Trade and Cooperation Agreement (TCA) concluded by the European Community with the Soviet Union in 1989, so a new bilateral economic agreement was long overdue. And although Minsk had awoken to the need to rationalise and reduce energy consumption, the EU's limited financial assistance in this domain had no real strategic impact. Meanwhile, the 2018 Convention on the legal status of the Caspian Sea brought new opportunities for energy projects with Kazakhstan (ones which circumvented Russia), but the EU had been slow to seize the moment.

Finally, Russia had shown a growing predilection for the use of cyber tools against its neighbours since 2007. Still, little was done to assist Belarus and Kazakhstan in terms of capacity building so that they could have detected intrusions and recovered more swiftly from major cyberattacks against national critical infrastructure. «

What can the West do to keep Russia in check, when the country's state policy is fundamentally at odds with the rules-based international order and when the Kremlin has every intention of continuing to act as a disruptive force?

ADDRESS RUSSIAN RULE-BREAKING.

TEXT: JAMES NIXEY

The Kremlin famously demands 'respect' from the world's leading powers and international organizations. [1] But it shows little respect itself for the rules-based international order. Indeed, it rejects the very notion that such an order exists. Where most Western governments see an imperfect liberal capitalist system – even one in retreat – Moscow's ruling elites see the slow passing of a hegemonic, US-led world order in which the 'rules' are slanted in the West's favour and Russia's 'natural rights' have been ignored. In this context, the Russian leadership does not consider its interests to lie in following others' rules. This presents a number of practical challenges for those in the West who nonetheless need to deter or respond to Russian aggression.

Russia has been perfectly clear that it wants a different international settlement, one in which no major decisions may be taken without its consent. Seeing itself (despite all evidence to the contrary) as an indispensable world power, Russia pursues a goal in the West that consists of re-achieving the uncoupling of western Europe from eastern and central Europe in order to restore a historic sphere of influence.

This inevitably means that the Kremlin's ambition is a threat to all those European countries that subscribe to the current order, police it, or aspire to be a part of it.

Reprint mit freundlicher Genehmigung von **Chatham House Expert Perspectives,** June 2019.

The material extent of that threat can be seen in the 13,000 deaths in Ukraine since the start of the conflict in 2014, [2] and in the tens of thousands more casualties in Syria, not to mention the unknown number of victims of covert Russian operations in the UK.

All can be interpreted as collateral damage from Moscow expressing its dissatisfaction with how the West thinks the world should be organized. A key point here is the importance of taking the consequences of Russia's foreign policy positioning seriously, rather than reducing it to a simple negotiable difficulty. Failure to respond appropriately to Moscow's declared ambitions will mean further assaults on Western societies, populations and democratic institutions.

THE COOPERATION ILLUSION

The seductive myth that there must be common ground for cooperation with Russia must be rebutted. Whereas the West may be able to cooperate artfully with China to strengthen the rules-based international order when mutual interests align, this will not work with Russia. China profited from the end of the Cold War, Russia lost everything. China wants to use the system to rise up within it. Russia's leadership, as mentioned, wants a different system altogether. [3]

Facing structural economic decline, Russia cannot fulfil its supposed great power destiny by any »

Western diplomacy could exploit Russia's relationship with China to drive a wedge between the two countries. Western engagement with China's Belt and Road Initiative, which bypasses Russia, could provide a clear example to Russia that the latter's interests lie in genuine cooperation not isolation.

means that are acceptable to the West. The Kremlin has correctly deduced that Russia's developmental prospects are so poor that the country cannot rise within the established rules of the international order.

In this context, the Kremlin understands 'cooperation' simply as a means to extract compromise and concession. In rare instances where Russia's interests coincide with those of the West, any mutual gains are entirely context-limited: the confluence of factors cannot be leveraged to achieve cooperation elsewhere.

In fact, the reverse mechanism applies, with Moscow exploiting any supposed magnanimity on a particular issue to advance its agenda in other areas. There are ample illustrations of how, when the West weakens or concedes, Moscow entrenches, reinforces tactical gains, and pushes further.

Above all, the search for common interests is of no help to those seeking to deter Russia's worst excesses. This is because those actions – from military interventions in Ukraine and Syria to digital interference in Western democratic processes – are designed to ensure that Russia's place at the top table is maintained. They are a fundamental element of state policy.

DUAL OPTIONS FOR RESPONSE

Defence of the West, its societies, institutions and populations, relies now as it long has done on strong but calibrated resistance to Moscow through a mixture of *deterrence by denial* and *deterrence by punishment*. Deterrence by denial means closing off the possibility of easy wins for Russia.

This entails a number of actions: investment in stronger financial regulation; political funding for transparency initiatives; [4] continued vigilance against Russian malign-influence operations; the observation of cyber hygiene; policies to ensure energy security and protect critical infrastructure (which should include legal systems); and a robust military posture. None of these steps definitively eliminate the Russian threat, but they incrementally diminish the country's ability to do harm.

Deterrence by punishment requires the West to impose costs and consequences where Russia violates international rules or norms. There is evidence (where information exists in the public domain) that holding at risk what Vladimir Putin cares about has worked on occasions. Economic sanctions are the most obvious example.

While there is debate over the precise extent of their effects – largely from people who dispute the justification for such measures in the first place – their symbolic value as an admonishment should not be understated. If in no other way, the effectiveness of sanctions can be measured by the urgency of the Russian elite's desire to have them removed.

However, sanctions are insufficient on their own, and in any event are not the only option for responding to Russian actions. Western commercial diplomacy could exploit Russia's friendly, if unequal, relationship with China to drive a wedge between the two countries. Cautious and appropriate Western engagement with China's Belt and Road Initiative, which bypasses Russia, could provide a clear example to Russia that the latter's interests lie in genuine cooperation not isolation.   »

A more forceful option includes proper enforcement of laws and regulations on responsible media behaviour. These laws, which already exist in most European countries, offer the potential to counter Russian propaganda and disinformation more effectively.

Outright bans of RT (formerly 'Russia Today') and Sputnik, the Kremlin's chief information outlets in the West, would likely be counterproductive: not only prompting tit-for-tat retaliation against Western broadcasters but also reflecting poorly on free-speech protections.

However, appropriate regulatory penalties could still induce both media organizations to substantially adjust their output and behaviour. [5] Regulators could bar Western advertisers from buying space on Russian channels. And temporary (but repeated) removal of broadcasts from the airwaves – as and when Russian news reporting breaches official standards of impartiality – would have some impact as a punishment and could boost conformity.

This should not be confused with 'winning' in the information warfare space, where Russia's authoritarian machinery gives it the edge. However, the West doesn't have to let Russia win quite so easily.

WHEN THEY GO LOW …

When resisting Russia, it is critical that the West not depart from its values to do so, since this would be self-defeating. One positive model is the package of legislation recently passed in Australia against subversive Chinese activity. Far from representing a departure from Western norms and values, many of the measures are aimed at increasing transparency.[6]

Education is also a fundamental part of the long-term answer. Threat perception is critical: populations need to understand that their countries have a Russia problem – or, more accurately, a problem with Russia's leadership. As ever, we can learn from the front-line states. Poland has ensured that its domestic Russia expertise has not faded away, unlike in so many other Western countries where capacity and language skills have been eroded. In the Nordic states, children are schooled to identify disinformation (fake news) from an early age.[7]

Above all, Western policymakers must be clear-sighted in recognizing that dealing with Russia requires persistence, a willingness to play the long game, and an appetite for bearing short-term economic and diplomatic retaliation and the domestic political fallout from it.

It also requires recognition that a firm response cannot and should not be reliant on full Western unity, which is unrealistic. This, too, underlines the need for sturdier EU diplomacy, not always a strong point under the current High Representative. While the immediate impacts of resisting Russia's ambition are likely to be uncomfortable, the long-term consequences – both for Europe and for the rules-based international order as a whole – of not doing so would be devastating. «

NOTES:

[1] In Russian geopolitical thinking, 'respect' is code for a demand that the West continue to respect the borders and rules that defined the USSR until 1991. This covers a further 2 million square miles of land, and an additional 140 million people, compared to modern Russia.

[2] Office of the United Nations High Commissioner for Human Rights (2019), *Report on the human rights situation in Ukraine, 16 November 2018 to 15 February 2019*, https://www.ohchr.org/Documents/Countries/UA/ReportUkraine16Nov2018-15Feb2019.pdf (accessed 22 May 2019).

[3] It should also be remembered that Russia possesses networks and local knowledge in central and eastern Europe that China does not.

[4] 'Sunlight is the best disinfectant,' said Louis Brandeis. Brandeis, L. (1914), *Other People's Money and How the Bankers Use It*.

[5] In the UK, the broadcasting regulator Ofcom repeatedly announces that it has 'sanctioned' RT. This is misleading, since the supposed sanctions are no more than warnings or notices of transgression.

[6] Hamilton, C. (2018), 'Australia's Fight Against Chinese Political Interference', *Foreign Affairs*, 26 July 2018, https://www.foreignaffairs.com/articles/australia/2018-07-26/australias-fight-against-chinese-political-interference.

[7] Mackintosh, E. (2019), 'Finland is winning the war on fake news. What it's learned may be crucial to Western democracy', CNN Special Report, May 2019, https://edition.cnn.com/interactive/2019/05/europe/finland-fake-news-intl/.

DIE REDAKTION EMPFIEHLT

Bruno Maçães

BELT AND ROAD. A CHINESE WORLD ORDER.

C Hurst & Co Publishers Ltd,
2018, 224 Seiten,
ISBN: 978-1-787-38002-8

„ What does the biggest geopolitical project of our time tell us about China's global ambitions?

China's Belt and Road strategy is acknowledged to be the most ambitious geopolitical initiative of the age. Covering almost seventy countries by land and sea, it will affect every element of global society, from shipping to agriculture, digital economy to tourism, politics to culture. Most importantly, it symbolises a new phase in China's ambitions as a superpower: to remake the world economy and crown Beijing as the nealisation.

Frederike Schotters

FRANKREICH UND DAS ENDE DES KALTEN KRIEGES. GEFÜHLSSTRATEGIEN DER ÉQUIPE MITTERRAND 1981-1990

De Gruyter Oldenbourg,
2019, 462 Seiten,
ISBN: 978-3-11-059741-7

„ In den 1980er Jahren entwickelte die équipe Mitterrand Ideen und Konzepte zu einer umfassenden Neustrukturierung der internationalen Staatenwelt. Erstmals werden in der Studie systematisch emotionshistorische Ansätze genutzt, um politische Handlungsstrategien zu erforschen. Durch die Weiterentwicklung methodischer Instrumentarien wird dargelegt, wie sich Emotionen im Kontext internationaler Beziehungen – in Außen- und Sicherheits- und Europapolitik – erforschen lassen.

David Rowan

NON-BULLSHIT INNOVATION. RADICAL IDEAS FROM THE WORLD'S SMARTEST MINDS

Bantam Press,
2019, 384 Seiten,
ISBN: 978-1-787-63119-9

„ David Rowan travels the globe in search of the most exciting and pioneering startups building the future. He's got to know the founders of WhatsApp, Google, Spotify, Twitter and countless other ambitious entrepreneurs disrupting businesses in almost every sector. And yet too often the companies they're disrupting don't get it. They think they can innovate through jargon: with talk of change agents and co-creation gurus, hackfests and pilgrimages to Silicon Valley. It's mostly pointless innovation theatre. But he's also discovered some transformative approaches to innovation, often in places you might least expect.

Ajay Agrawal, Joshua Gans & Avi Goldfarb

PREDICTION MACHINES: THE SIMPLE ECONOMICS OF ARTIFICIAL INTELLIGENCE

Harvard Business Review,
2018, 250 Seiten,
ISBN: 978-1-633-69567-2

„ Penetrating, fun, and always insightful and practical, Prediction Machines follows its inescapable logic to explain how to navigate the changes on the horizon. The impact of AI will be profound, but the economic framework for understanding it is surprisingly simple.

In Prediction Machines, three eminent economists recast the rise of AI as a drop in the cost of prediction. With this single, masterful stroke, they lift the curtain on the AI-is-magic hype and show how basic tools from economics provide clarity about the AI revolution and a basis for action by CEOs, managers, policy makers, investors, and entrepreneurs.

Jenny Andersson

THE FUTURE OF THE WORLD. FUTUROLOGY, FUTURISTS, AND THE STRUGGLE FOR THE POST COLD WAR IMAGINATION.

Oxford University Press, 2018, 288 Seiten, ISBN: 978-0-198-81433-7

❞ The Future of the World is devoted to the intriguing field oThe Future of the World is devoted to the intriguing field of study which emerged after World War Two, futurism or futurology. Jenny Andersson explains how futurist scholars and researchers imagined the Cold War and post Cold War world and the tools and methods they would use to influence and change that world.

Using unexplored archival collections, The Future of the World reconstructs the Cold War networks of futurologists and futurists.

Heidi J. S. Tworek

NEWS FROM GERMANY. THE COMPETITION TO CONTROL WORLD COMMUNICATIONS, 1900–1945.

Harvard University Press, 2019, 344 Seiten, ISBN: 978-0-674-98840-8

❞ To control information is to control the world. This innovative history reveals how, across two devastating wars, Germany attempted to build a powerful communication empire.

Information warfare may seem like a new feature of our contemporary digital world. But it was just as crucial a century ago, when the great powers competed to control and expand their empires. In News from Germany, Heidi Tworek uncovers how Germans fought to regulate information at home and used the innovation of wireless technology to magnify their power abroad.

Zsuzsa Anna Ferenczy

EUROPE, CHINA, AND THE LIMITS OF NORMATIVE POWER.

Edward Elgar Publishing, 2019, 192 Seiten, ISBN: 978-1-78897-581-0

❞ Europe, China, and the Limits of Normative Power is a groundbreaking book, offering insights into European influence regarding China's development, during a period when Europe confronts its most serious political, social, and economic crises of the post-war period. Considering Europe's identity and its future international relevance, this book examines the extent to which Europe's multi-layered governance structure, the normative divergence overshadowing EU–China relations and Europe's crises continue to shape – and often limit – Europe's capacity to inspire China's development.

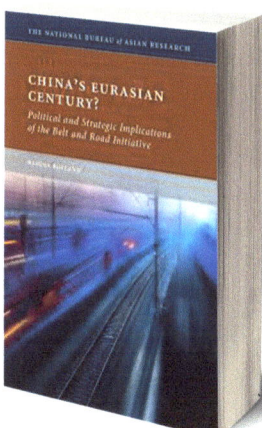

Nadège Rolland

CHINA'S EURASIAN CENTURY? POLITICAL AND STRATEGIC IMPLICATIONS OF THE BELT AND ROAD INITIATIVE.

The National Bureau of Asian Research, 2017, 208 Seiten, ISBN: 978-1-93913-150-8

❞ Drawing mostly from the work of Chinese official and analytic communities who are striving to make Belt and Road Initiative (BRI) a reality, this study examines the concept's origins, drivers, and various component parts, as well as the accompanying ideational narrative and domestic and international objectives, as seen through Beijing's eyes. More than a mere list of revamped infrastructure projects, BRI is a grand strategy that advances China's goal of establishing itself as the preponderant power in Eurasia and a global power second to none.

Bildserie „Brave New World 1984" © наталья / pexels

Infrastructure projects, imperial ambitions, and international status were firmly intertwined for many Germans by 1900. Communications were part of this global competition to further imperialism through infrastructure. The development of new wireless communications technology also made air a third dimension of global power alongside land and sea.

A WORLD WIRELESS NETWORK ::
German Ambitions by 1900.

TEXT: HEIDI J. S. TWOREK

German officials only began to pay sustained attention to communications infrastructure around 1900. From the first successful transatlantic submarine cable in 1866, an oligopoly of Anglo-American companies dominated the global laying of submarine cables. Submarine telegraphy spread rapidly, reaching Asia, Australia, and South America by the late 1870s. The German government did not even intervene to support the Siemens Brothers when they attempted to compete with the Anglo-American Eastern and Associated Companies in the 1870s.[1] Other nations were similarly acquiescent to a privately-run global system. The privately-owned Anglo-American submarine cables formed the basis for international cooperation that was regulated from 1865 by the International Telegraph Union (ITU). Crucially, though, the ITU never secured agreement from its members on protocols for communication during wars.[2]

From the 1890s, increasing German discontent with the role of news in politics and trade intertwined with growing unease about communications technology. If Germany was an imperial and global power, then it needed the accoutrements like cables. Competition

Textauszug: *News from Germany. The Competition to Control World Communications, 1900 – 1945;* Harvard University Press, Cambridge, 2019;

over cables was not just an expression of geopolitical rivalries. Rather, it was a battle over the information flows that undergirded imperial and global exchanges.

By 1908, German military officials became increasingly convinced that the British had plans for wireless domination to complement their cable network. General Helmuth von Moltke the Younger, chief of the general staff, devoted multiple memoranda and committee meetings to discussing the British-based Marconi Company's purported plans to erect large wireless stations around the world. Moltke emphasized that the first nation to transmit wireless around the world would gain significant military and political advantages.

Alongside Moltke's pleas from the military perspective, Kaiser Wilhelm II and other ministers invested in wireless for geopolitical and technological reasons. The German government intervened in private enterprise to create Telefunken, the main competitor to Marconi.

Telefunken soon produced an innovation called the quenched spark system that it implemented in 1909. The quenched spark system (or spark gap transmission) created an electrical oscillation through electrical sparks and transmitted information through Morse code. Wireless was a swifter means to counter British submarine cables around the world; it also helped »

German business to innovate. It was no coincidence that Guglielmo Marconi shared his 1909 Nobel Prize for innovation in wireless telegraphy with the German Karl Ferdinand Braun. Innovation in wireless technology formed part of a long-term German vision for infrastructural and informational independence centred around news agencies.

Fears about other nations constantly accelerated German plans. In July 1911, Molke reported to the Colonial Office that the French were looking into creating a world wireless network too.[3] French officials also aggressively subsidized and supported a strategy to lay cables to connect the French empire and counteract British influence.[4] The German government worked with the French to lay a cable to South America, in return for German help with France's network in West Africa. By 1913, Germany possessed 8.3 percent of the world's cables, while Britain still held a mighty 54.3 percent.[5]

More worryingly, multiple sources claimed that Marconi was working with the British postmaster general to erect a British-controlled "all-red line of wireless towers"[6]. A British network seemed dangerous for economic as well as political and military reasons. Marconi devices could not communicate with Telefunken devices, because Marconi had originally constructed his wireless as a closed, incompatible system. If Marconi succeeded, he would create a wireless monopoly.

Telefunken saw an opportunity. The company could exploit the German Colonial Office's fears about British use of wireless. On an enormous map, Telefunken officials drew the planned Marconi routes around the world. In a different colour on the same map, Telefunken sketched an alternative German route that it could create with government subsidies. If the British were planning a world wireless network, the Germans just had to preempt them.

After 1912 these fears receded. The Titanic disaster, however, pushed governments toward safety regulations. A radiotelegraphic conference in London in 1912 mandated that all ships with over fifty passengers install wireless receivers. The imperative of safety enabled Telefunken to break Marconi's monopoly: all ships were now legally obliged to be able to communicate with each other. By 1912, Marconi and Telefunken had agreed to exchange patents and only 294 of the 1554 ship stations did not belong to Telefunken or Marconi.[7] The market looked more like a duopoly than the oligopolistic cable market.[8]

The Anglo-American oligopoly over cables continued, as cable-laying proved expensive and time-consuming. At the same time then, Germans turned to wireless technology to bypass the British-dominated network altogether. From its emergence around 1900, perceived political, economic, and military needs shaped the development of wireless. Many did not see the need for wireless on land, because there was such a dense telegraph network already. In Germany, however, wireless promised to undermine the infrastructural premise of the news cartel: a submarine cable network dominated by Great Britain. «

NOTES
1) Simone M. Müller (2016). Wiring the World: The Social and Cultural Creation of Global Telegraph Networks; CUP, New York, Ch.2
2) Simone Müller (2015). Beyond the Means of 99 Percent of the Pouplation: Business Interests, State Intervention, and Submarine Telegraphy; Journal of Policy History, 27(3), pp. 439-464
3) Report from chief of the army general staff to Colonial Office, July 1911, BArch R1001/7198, p. 26
4) Pascal Griset (1996). "Enterprise, technologie et souveraineté. les télécommunications transatlantiques de la France", XIXe-XXe siècles; Paris, Editions rive droite
5) Max Röscher (1911). "Das Weltkabelnetz", Archiv für Post und Telegraphie 12, p.383
6) Report from German consulate in Sydney, July 26, 1911 and report from German Foreign Office, October 31, 1911, BArch R1001/7198, pp. 37-38 and 50-51
7) October 11, 1921, Hansard, column 680. See Stathis Arapostathis and Graeme Gooday (2013). Pattently Contestable: Electrical Technologies and Inventor Identities on Trial in Britain; Cambridge, MA, MIT Press, ch. 6
8) Winseck and Pike assert that the major communications companies cooperated from 1860 to 1930 rather than engaging in imperial competition. Dwayne Winseck and Robert Pike (2007). "Communication and Empire: Media, Markets, and Globalization, 1860-1930"; Durham, NC, Duke University Press; Yet this ignores the German government subsidies of Telefunken and German attempts to undermine cooperation.

I'm standing at the far end of an enclosed Pier 9 on San Francisco's Embarcadero. This pier is where a thirty-seven-year-old software company called Autodesk runs a 2,500-square-metre research lab and fabrication workshop to help it discover, and then prototype, the future. Today it's playing with industrial robots to learn how filmmakers might use them – if only the robots were simpler to program. Autodesk makes Maya, the visual effects and animation software favoured by countless Oscar-winners, so it has a vested interest in understanding how its customers might want to use it to film with robots. Besides, if its tools can help filmmakers effortlessly program robots, imagine the wider industrial applications of a frictionless robotics operating system. What if future Autodesk software could effectively liberate robots to better serve their human overlords?

FIND YOUR BLIND SPOTS.
A software giant reimagines manufacturing

TEXT: DAVID ROWAN

Erin Bradner, the Autodesk research scientist who runs the robotics lab, explains that the spaceship was hand-made for today's shoot by a collaborator at Industrial Light & Magic, the visual effects company founded by George Lucas to work on Star Wars. 'This is not a typical day in the robot lab,' she says with a grin as she watches the improvised shoot. The shoot is part of an experiment, she explains, to understand how Autodesk's existing software – it is a world leader in computer-aided design and 3D visual effects – could be adapted to make robots more easily controllable.

The standard way to program the robots would be to move each arm manually and slowly, and record each step using a hand-held control called a teach pendant. Here, by contrast, the team has pre-programmed both

Textauszug aus: Non-Bullshit Innovation. Radical Ideas from the World's Smartest Minds; Bantam Press, 2019;

arms with a version of Maya that automatically and instantly generates robot code simply from their start and end positions. The software, working from these two instructions, ensures that the robot moves smoothly and quickly along its six axes without the need for any human intervention. That saves huge amounts of time – and lets the software define the path that to a film camera seems most lifelike.

'Robots are typically programmed to do highly deterministic tasks in inflexible environments, but we want to unbolt them from the floor, metaphorically and physically, and get them to function on unstructured tasks in unstructured environments,' Bradner says, excitedly, as the robots dance in cinematic harmony. So what's actually an animation tool – Maya helps artists build a time-based sequence if shown a start and end drawing – is now able to give robots intuitive movements. In » other words, the animation software has been hacked to solve a problem it was never designed for. The endgame, Bradner explains, is to transform how humans work with robots, not just for filming, but for manufacturing. 'Toyota has its robot whisperers – the revered gentlemen who come in to program the robots, so that the rest of the factory can pick up the mantle. But what if the rest of us could approach that domain with less expertise, less mysticism? What if we could create real robot-human collaboration?'

This matters to Autodesk, because Autodesk makes software for the people who make our physical world. Architects, engineers and the construction industry design, model and build with products such as AutoCAD and Revit; industrial manufacturers prototype and scale production with Fusion 360 and Autodesk Inventor; infrastructure providers rely on Civil 3D and InfraWorks. There are Autodesk products for digital prototyping and injection-moulding simulation; for home tinkerers and amateur makers; and, as we've seen, for movie rendering and visual effects.

'If you've ever driven a high-performance car, admired a towering skyscraper, used a smartphone, or watched a great film,' as the company brochure puts it, 'chances are you've experienced what millions of Autodesk customers are doing with our software.' Yet this is a $30 billion company born in 1982 during the last great computing-platform transition, from mainframes to desktop PCs. It understands that the old rules won't keep it relevant during the current transition to cloud services, artificial intelligence and decentralized networks. So it has been aggressively searching for a sustainable and profitable role in this unpredictable future.

Autodesk knows it must turn from a legacy business, selling software in boxes, to an agile enabler of emerging manufacturing processes. And that this may involve helping tomorrow's clients design nano-factories, write DNA, empower robots . . . or whatever else comes next. Autodesk's answer to these challenges is to search relentlessly for its 'unknown unknowns' – to invest heavily and consistently in what Jeff Kowalski, its recently departed chief technology officer, calls 'discovering our blind spots'.

Out of total revenues of $1.5 to $2 billion in recent years, it has typically dedicated $700 to $750 million to R&D. For Kowalski, those letters stand for 'risk and determinism': while most of the company pursues the deterministic goals of pleasing today's shareholders, the CTO's office funds longer-term, riskier experiments in machine learning, material and life sciences, digital manufacturing, artists' fellowships, and wherever else it identifies knowledge gaps. 'You and I don't have very different jobs,' Kowalski confides to me over a beer. 'We go out and explore and talk to people, and we start piecing things together. My team does the science, makes the prototypes, and brings further-out speculation to customers to explore. This company got really good at shipping known product with known resources – we've been around for ever. The problem is, what do you put at the front end of the machine tomorrow?'

That explains why I've come to Pier 9, where as well as the robotics lab Autodesk runs a reconfigurable micro-factory, an advanced fabrication lab, a 3D-print studio, Instructables training courses, resident artists' workspaces, and a hybrid pool of talent hired to push the boundaries of digital manufacturing. I'm given a leisurely tour by Mickey McManus, an accomplished and intellectually curious industrial designer who has ten patents and co-wrote the book Trillions: Thriving in the Emerging Information Ecology. Kowalski, CTO for twelve years from 2006, brought in McManus as an Autodesk Fellow, a part-time role designed to challenge the leadership with provocative ideas. Which he certainly does.

McManus talks quickly, thoughtfully, and with a stream of radical notions that take me a while to digest. As we walk past a giant metal-cutting water jet, a vast laser-cutter and an electronics lab, he explains the pier's new experimental, AIdependent micro-factory. 'What if you flip the design of a factory so you don't know what it will build tomorrow? What if it just dreams overnight, learning in the cloud how to make a new product based on market demand, and then reformats itself in the morning to produce it?' My eyes widen. «

The idea of taking on societal responsibility as a trust-building measure in symmetrical communication of values, that is actually is not particularly new, nor is there an immediate causal link to the financial crisis. Rather, there is a good case to believe that had the economy begun to take responsibility seriously prior to 2007 and acted accordingly, the world may have been spared the crisis. Whatever the case may be, with business-English terms like "corporate citizenship" (CC), "corporate social responsibility" (CSR), "corporate responsibility" (CR), "corporate sustainability," "sustainability," "transparency" or "good citizen," this concept has also found its way into the morality programs, management circles, media, and some academic disciplines in the German-speaking world since the 1990s.

THE EMERGENCE OF CORPORATE CITIZENSHIP

TEXT: WOLFGANG LAMPRECHT

Despite all the terminological confusion, there is a common-sense agreement on what the factor of corporate citizenship means, namely values, such as down-to-earthness, tradition, social and ecological responsibility, culture, morality, security, and employee pension plans, as they relate to the role of corporations in society, and that it exerts a positive influence on stakeholders and brings about calculable successes (cf. Schönborn, 2008, p. 99). Today, corporations are almost universally seen as an integral element of society – regardless of the respective chosen concept of contemporary corporate leadership. Of course, in the close reciprocal connection of society and economy, change processes play an important role. Hence, changes in society implant themselves into corporations and confront them with new tasks. And vice versa. Against the backdrop of fundamental transformations of society and overall economic conditions, the management of corporations was and is faced with entirely new challenges regarding increased competition.

CONNOTATIVE DEFINITIONS OF CORPORATE CITIZENSHIP

Corporate citizenship, as a company's ethical self-image, therefore denotes an ideal model relationship between citizens, government, and corporations. With a view towards the common good, the corporation contributes its resources and capabilities to the social and political process and thus defines rights and obligations »

Unloading goods beside a river, ca. 1905 © Oliver Hulme Collection / University of Bristol - Historical Photographs of China

as a morally proactive citizen (cf. Wieland, 2001). The corporate citizenship concept stresses the aspect of companies assuming responsibility in the sense of a sustainable development of society, as a part of which companies, of course, see themselves (cf. Schwalbach/ Schwerk, 2008, p. 79).

Corporate social responsibility or *corporate responsibility* defines a management guided by values and norms for the purpose of a voluntary, solidarity-based solution to societal problems in the respective environment of a corporate citizen. With CSR/CR as an important aspect of stakeholder communication, concepts and measures are implemented – partly in cooperation with partners – which help solve humanitarian, social, cultural, ecological or educational problems (cf. ibid.) and produce a verifiable return, in whatever form. Available measures include corporate giving, corporate sponsorship, corporate volunteering, corporate investments, et-

cetera. Ultimately, it is up to *corporate social communication* to transparently convey *corporate social performance*.

A company thus achieves *sustainability*, meaning the famous and much-cited *sustainability*. Its definition (beyond environmental protection issues) is the long-term continued existence of a system – in due consideration of the needs and expectations of stakeholders as well as a company's current values-oriented goals – centered on balanced economic, ecological, cultural, and social development born of the responsibility towards future generations (cf. ebd).

How the needs and interests of all stakeholders are balanced and ultimately defined, communicated, and made manageable, so as to avoid negative effects on a company's competitiveness, that is the task of *corporate governance*, at least according to the European approach. It advances (as opposed to the Anglo-American ap-

> Thus far, the discussion around and about corporate social responsibility has frequently skated over, but has hardly really addressed and articulated the issue of culture. It is still rarely conceived of as a field that urgently needs to be given ample space ...

proach) not only the owner's interests, but has a positive effect on all stakeholders.

A company is therefore a social institution that raises the prosperity of all stakeholders, including its owners. Good corporate governance contributes to speedy conflict resolution and is therefore conducive to corporate success. Consequently, a corporation's societal responsibility is inseparably linked to good corporate governance. The corresponding set of regulations, which is to say the principles and conduct a corporation has agreed upon in the context of corporate governance, are explained in its *code of conduct* (cf. Schwalbach/Schwerk, 2008, P. 82f), observance of legal provisions and guidelines as well as its transparent communication is settled under *compliance*. It is thus a constituent element of CSR.

Now that we have normatively defined the corporate citizen complex in this manner, this renders irrelevant the cultural factors, different social fallback systems, and market forms as the ostensive parameters of the definition of CSR. When it comes to details, it is the measures that decide. They must of course be applied in a diversified manner. Accordingly, the measures of CSR are understood as communicative acts, and in more ways than one. First, of course committing to social/cultural responsibility with the intention of generating trust only makes sense when it is done publicly, which is to say with the involvement of public audiences. On the other hand, measures taken by a corporate citizen within CSR as communicative and (media) transmitted acts are per se a statement and, being realized through various communication channels, acts of mass communication. They must not only be assessed from a systems theory and a qualitative perspective, as well as with regard to their effect, but also in economical terms; and thus should also be understood, per se, as a business process.

CORPORATE CULTURAL RESPONSIBILITY

Especially the crises after 2008 have directed attention in public discussions to a form of responsibility where corporations voluntarily become engaged in the solution of societal problems. In the process, the term CSR (corporate social responsibility) as a principle of communicative action has enormously increased in importance (in the interest of credibility, don't just talk the talk, walk the walk, too). Thus far, the discussion around and about corporate social responsibility has frequently skated over, but has hardly really addressed and articulated the issue of culture. It is still rarely conceived of as a field that urgently needs to be given ample space within the as yet young discipline of CSR. Because in the context of CSR, corporate cultural responsibility (CCR) expresses nothing less than the cultural responsibility of corporations for culture. CCR is also part of a corporation's social responsibility.

The term *corporate cultural responsibility* was actually coined in 2002 in the context of a workshop jointly held by SIEMENS Arts Program and the economics faculty at Witten/Herdecke University, but has not arrived at the communication departments of corporations themselves, as yet. On the contrary, at Deutsche Bank, for example, CCR is defined in fuzzy terminology and conducted as "cultural sponsorship in the context of corporate citizenship," namely even outside of the communications department. This can nevertheless count as progress, as most corporations still work with the term arts or *cultural sponsorship*. Presently, the notion of corporate cultural responsibility is not very widespread.

According to Beate Hentschel and Michael Hutter who coined the term, corporate cultural responsibility raises the question as to the background, meaning, and benefit of the cultivation of cultural environ- »

Sampans and harbourside shops, Hong Kong, 1925 © University of Bristol - Historical Photographs of China

ments by corporations, and thus the responsibility of corporations for a lively and potent cultural environment. CCR is thus defined as a "good citizen" (derivative of corporate citizenship) setting the focus of CSR on cultural engagement and, beyond plain old communication, comprising "a corporation's internal and external cultural engagement, including promotion and qualification of employees, pitching cultural events or sponsorship and patronage." This approach has decisive advantages. At first, cultural engagement does not directly seem to be part of a company's core business. Furthermore, the position is not called into question that a corporation's essential tasks consist in providing high quality and highly sustainable products and services at the best possible price and to generate profits. But in the sense of precisely this corporate self-interest, it is essential to understand that living corporate responsibility via its stakeholders on the basis of cultural governance is part of the self-preservation that determines

success. It is thus simply a part of corporate governance to ensure that a company's stakeholders fare well, in particular customers, employees, investors, owners, etcetera. The reason being that "good capitalism" only becomes possible through participative engagement with the issues relevant to society. Now, that really is something art incessantly brings up.

HOW ART BENEFITS THE ECONOMY

According to Max Weber's interpretation of the term, economic activity must be designed in such a way that economic services, goods and products are not only based on the fulfillment of consumer needs, but must be desired, and that for this desire to take shape, welfare and provision for old age must be secured (Weber 1976, p. 31ff). This can result in innovations, product design, marketing, and corporate communication, but also in social relationships, which are appreciated as

… every artist, every work of art, and every art event works to be recognized as deserving of these titles. In a mediatized society, it is impressive to witness this competency in communicative competition for attention.

sources of a present or future potential power of control over services as well as providing economic opportunities (ibid., p. 34). Furthermore, Weber's definition also means that in the interest of sustainability, which he saw at its basis early on, corporations in their own economic interest need to help in ensuring that society fares well. It is only in a society that wants products, goods, and services it can also afford that a corporation can survive. Economy and society thus certainly appear to be communicating vessels.

Drawing a connection to the role of art and culture – leaving aside philosophical and sociological contemplation of the constitutive necessity of a civilized, value-based society for a company's core business – of course, to begin with, social relationships are a topic of interest. Cultural and art events have always been used, for example, as an indirectly profitable communication platform for initial business contacts, to solidify business relations or to enhance the attractiveness of business locations. Thanks to art's inherent ability to reflect on society and its issues, it served as both condensed and visionary foundational and market research towards the presentation of developments, fashions, and trends. And, particularly against the backdrop of globalization, also to take stock of the cultural socialization and identity in which a corporation has to act.

Finally, artifacts communicate demonstrative power, standing, and (life) style and to this day are regarded as an object of desire (which benefits the economy). They have always served as evidence of prestige and image, as coded identifiers of perfect success and, in giving an example, incentives to emulate the owner/commissioner. Collectors (including those of recordings, books, antiques, etcetera) are seen as opinion leaders, as visionaries who change a society not only on the level of everyday business life, but, with their passion, frequently also on that of the formation of taste. As trend setters, they discover new styles, shape the world of art and culture and move markets for exceptional products. Sometimes by using art and design objects as investment objects.

Since time unknown, works of art have inspired, motivated, given wings, brought peace and happiness to stakeholders. And they have contributed to social balance, innovation, creation of value, growth, and prosperity, which, as part of the cyclical movement of economy and art, in turn exerts a positive effect on art itself – and thus attracts artists. Such a "concentration of artists" generally produces an agglomeration of experimentation, experience, and knowledge that generates a fertile soil not only with regard to tolerance, taste, and life style. It is, above all, a boon to civilized behavior and creativity in social environments. Furthermore, every artist, every work of art, and every art event works to be recognized as deserving of these titles. In a mediatized society, it is impressive to witness this competency in communicative competition for attention. What will be crucial for an all-round balanced society of the 21st century is the realization that – on our way from an industrial society to one based on services and knowledge, from an employment to an activity and risk based society – creativity, mobility, and flexibility (genuine competency of artistic creativity) have become key factors in global competition (cf. Rothauer, 2005). This is felt in everyone's daily life. There are, for example, no more old-style bank employees in banking, there are customer advisors and financial consultants whose capital is »

Boats on the Huangpu River, Shanghai, 1930 © Billie Love Historical Collection / University of Bristol - Historical Photographs of China

knowledge, know-how, creativity, and communication skills. The technical part of financial transactions is now largely taken care of, across national borders, by machines or automated (communication) processes.

Ultimately, this is also about the theory which states that a person's knowledge, abilities, skills, and behavior cannot be separated from him or her. In economics, this is called human capital, intellectual resources, and an intangible asset, which is also reflected in a corporate brand, the brand value (cf. Lamprecht, 2013, p. 219ff). In the interest of a corporation's productivity and society's prosperity, of course that capital ought to be increased (cf. Towse, 2004, p. 6ff). This even touches on the core tasks of CCR.

Let's leave aside for a moment the indirect creation of value that is generally expected of art, which increases a corporation's range of activity and improves the internal and external quality of life connected with it through aesthetic, entertainment, and communicative values, keeping people open to discourse, flexible, and creative. Let's also leave aside the direct creation of economic value through cultural economic externalities (options value, existence value, bequest value, prestige value, educational values; cf. Lamprecht 2013, p. 215). There is one aspect that has featured ever more prominently in the discussion on the relationship between economy and art: Many of the hopes for future economic prosperity pinned on sectors of the creative industries are inconceivable without art and culture.

As long as financing of this guiding principle seemed secure, the notion that culture is also a basic pattern of the economy could be regarded as mainstream thinking. But it seems to become obsolete to the degree that a crisis forces cost cutting …

Culture is dependent on the economy and the economy is dependent on culture, and culture itself is an important sector of the economy, a motor of its creativity, and a boon to the attractiveness of locations and images (cf. Wagner 2010, p. 20ff). That is why many potentials of the principle of corporate cultural sponsorship of the mutual transfer of culture, goods, and knowledge are still waiting to be tapped.

The above-described model has one crucial advantage. It lies in the fact that within CCR, unlike in the past, we no longer have to polish and perpetuate the well-worn terminological separation (of the CCR measures) of sponsorship, patronage, donation campaigns, etcetera as a prerequisite for business legitimization of individual cultural sponsorship measures. We can now look at individual measures as additive in the context of an overarching CCR idea and communication strategy.

CONCEPTUAL SUMMARY

Now, cultural engagement is actually not part of the core business of commercial enterprises. Furthermore, the standpoint is not called into question that a corporation's essential tasks consist in providing high quality and highly sustainability products and services at the best possible price, and to generate profit. However, precisely in the sense of this corporate self-interest, it is essential to understand that activities outside of its classic core business, which is to say living corporate responsibility and thereby incurring costs, are part of the self-preservation that determines success; the more so as a company's stakeholders – above all customers, employees, investors, and the public – have, for several years now, become better organized and more influential with regard to the role expected of corporations. Consequently, self-preservation certainly needs to be understood as part of the core business – especially when agency of the media plays a major role in the process.

Aside from cultural criticism, the problem is this: As long as financing of this guiding principle seemed secure, the notion that culture is also a basic pattern of the economy could be regarded as mainstream thinking. But it seems to become obsolete to the degree that a crisis forces cost cutting, successes are no longer achieved and verifiable as desired, and this devaluation can even create a maelstrom that gets in the way of a growth perspective. The suspicion suggests itself that cultural studies and social sciences far too often choose as their subject the economy, and in economics, only business studies focus on culture. So far, the central question from a capitalist point of view (ultimately also when it comes, for instance, to classic sponsorship as sales and brand communication) has always been what the economy can do for culture; and rather less what culture can do for the economy.

For a company, the concept of corporate citizenship means nothing less than the internalization of the business ethics of "good citizens," which gives visibility to a responsible conduct towards a society and its future. Especially the crises after 2008 have directed attention in public discussions to such a form of responsibility. In the process, the concept of corporate responsibility as a principle of communicative action has greatly gained in importance. The objective is still: against the backdrop of a massive loss of confidence in the face of saturated markets and similar products, corporations competing for customers are forced to approach their stakeholders on different than usual paths. CCR entails the wish to set a company apart from the competition and to secure trust, completive advantages, and a verifiable return, especially in the area of corporate communication. »

With its current group exhibition of international contemporary art, *Tomorrow is the Question*, the art museum ARoS in Aarhus, Denmark, spotlights humanity's collective future. The goal is to invite the audience to "reflection and discussion of present and future challenges", as it says in the exhibition's catalogue, and it is obvious that the climate challenge carries considerable weight. A highly visible entrance exhibit, a burning red neon Earth, is created by Mona Hatoum and refers among other things to the UN's 17 global goals for sustainable development.

ART, THE FUTURE, AND THE DUAL GAZE

TEXT: MORTEN GRØNBORG

Tomorrow is the Question is created in collaboration between curator Luise Faurschou and ARoS under the leadership of director Erlend Høyersten and has several of the characteristics that have placed the museum and its exhibitions among the most visited in Scandinavia: It exhibits works that the audience remembers and often can interact with and which they share on social media, which makes more people come to see and be a part of the exhibition. The most notable work in the current exhibition is a digital waterfall, an installation created by Japanese teamLab, which takes up the rear walls and the entire floor in a large room. The audience can interact with the installation, which registers their movements and turns the waterfall into flowers gathering around people.

First and foremost, the exhibition is very well curated, which makes it the real piece of art. Despite notable works and great names among the exhibiting artists, it is mainly the theme and exhibition as such that form the centrepiece, which bears witness to a certain artistic and curatorial confidence.

zuerst erschienen in: **Scenario Magazin**, Mai 19, 3 / 2019; http://www.scenariomagazine.com

FUTURE AND ART

We meet Erlend Høyersten on the opening day of *Tomorrow is the Question*, shortly before the opening itself, as he has set time aside to talk with us and have pictures taken. I have briefed him in advance that he should expect to be interviewed, show us around the exhibition, and be ready to stand in front of the camera while doing this, all over the course of three hours. Høyersten takes all this in his stride and with great empathy, despite the demanding working conditions for a man who shortly after will play host to several hundred guests. While we take the first pictures, I ask him to tell us about the fundamental idea behind the exhibition.

Why does a museum dedicated to modern and contemporary art put the future on the agenda?

"The exhibition is in a way a natural follow-up to earlier projects we've had, which in various ways circled around the fact that mankind for the first time ever is facing a collective future. In the past, mankind's future wasn't collective, but diverse, shaped by geography and social conditions. Today, however, we are all affected by the global climate challenge" he answers. »

I believe that mankind has always felt special no matter what age we have lived in – but we are now in a period and a situation where the future plays an entirely different role than in the past. In the 1960s, 1970s, and 1980s, we grew up with the idea that the world could be taken hold of. When I see young people today, they do not have the same opportunity for dreaming.

WHAT ART DOES

Høyersten refers to the museum's major commitment, *The Garden*, a triennial held in 2017 with the subheading *End of Times, Beginning of Time*. Here, the focus was on mankind's understanding or misunderstanding of nature over the last 400 years, divided according to past, present, and future, exhibiting works by a range of international visual artists, including a range of large installations and new commissioned works. The triennial had exhibits at the museum, around the city of Aarhus, and out in nature, along the coast. The most discussed and provocative work was no doubt German artist Katharina Grosse's location-specific happening where she painted an area in a park – including a whole tree, parts of the road and a bicycle path, and a large swath of grass – bright pink and white with acrylic paint.

"The Garden was also about the future with a focus on the Anthropocene (our current geological age, where traces of human activity can be seen in geological layers; ed.). I believe that mankind has always felt special no matter what age we have lived in – but we are now in a period and a situation where the future plays an entirely different role than in the past. In the 1960s, 1970s, and 1980s, we grew up with the idea that the world could be *taken hold of*. When I see young people today, they do not have the same opportunity for dreaming. They learn that the world must be saved. There has been a mental shift, and it may be the true generation gap between young and older people today," Høyersten says.

What, then is the role of art? What is it capable of in relation to the future's special status or role in our times?

"Art plays a very special role in relation to what is coming. Artists' imagination, their ability for lateral and radical thinking and for breaking things up are important to our society. There is a lot of talk about disruption now, particularly in business circles. It may seem a bit pretentious to use that word about an art museum, but art has always been disruptive. Disturb, disturb, disturb! That is what art does. With art and artists, we are given the opportunity as the audience of the work – and sometimes as participants in and co-creators of the work – for training our cognitive flexibility, the ability to interact with others, and the ability to set yourself into other people's perspectives; i.e., our empathy. That is what art can do."

Let us for a moment return to what you said about generational differences. It seems that you see a shift from a development perspective to a survival perspective in young people's worldview. Is this why the exhibition has more dystopian than utopian works?

"You could say that, yes. Dystopian worlds aren't nice, so we often turn our backs on them, since we can't grasp their consequences. They can seem too abstract and complex. However, what art can do is precisely to articulate taboos; through art you can grasp and talk about difficult things. You may not sit at home over dinner and talk about the climate crisis or genocide, but you can do that at a museum. Yet we also have utopian works among the exhibits, and »

I am not the only one who has deactivated my Facebook, and I think that people soon would rather once again meet at a bar instead of being on Tinder or Grindr. We have believed that the digital has been the solution, and it is, of course – for one thing I wouldn't want to do without my phone to guide me.

overall, our approach is open. After all, the exhibition is called *Tomorrow is the Question*."

Why is the exhibition called this? What is the meaning of the title?

"It derives from Rirkrit Tiravenija's work of the same name (a row of ping-pong tables set up outside of the exhibition as such, with the printed words: TOMORROW IS THE QUESTION; ed.). His ping-pong tables may be described as relational aesthetics, where the audience literally must play along and become cocreators. What I think is so cool is that anybody can play pingpong and hit with the bat, and that is the idea of all this; that the future is collective. The exhibition was originally initiated by Luise Faurschou, and she included that work very early. And then it just hit me during our collective work that the exhibition should be called the same as this work, precisely because the questions we ask today provide the answers for tomorrow."

Hence the title refers indirectly to that future challenges should be solved collectively – and that a museum could be a platform for that?

"Yes, collectively. Often when coming to a museum, you act as if you have entered a church – you don't sit on the floor, you show a sort of piousness, you don't run, and above all, you mustn't laugh. But with a work like Tiravenijas', we make the audience relax and be together, and I believe that is hugely important. Solitude and estrangement are growing problems in our society, and in many ways, we lack places to come together. Instead, we have got cells or echo chambers that each of us sit in."

Are you thinking of the idea that we live in digital filter bubbles where we are only fed that we already know or like because the algorithms have taught us what we would like to have?

"Yes. We lack places where we can have the collective conversation. It wasn't like that before. However, times change in a sort of pendulum motion where we react to whatever a time represents and create a new time. The Age of Enlightenment e.g. came about as a response to a deeply religious period. And I also see signs of a counter-reaction today; a counter-reaction to the quick and the digital. I am not the only one who has deactivated my Facebook, and I think that people soon would rather once again meet at a bar instead of being on Tinder or Grindr. We have believed that the digital has been the solution, and it is, of course – for one thing I wouldn't want to do without my phone to guide me. Even so, I sense that people want to return to something else, something quieter. I just read in The Guardian that youths under 30 don't go to mindfulness or yoga, but in fact go to art museums to find peace."

AUTHORITY

It is interesting that you mention it, as what I experience in our cultural life today is the opposite approach to audiences – that museums and theatres do everything they can to catch people's attention, so they don't rapidly zap on, because boredom has become forbidden. What do you think about this?

"There has been a period where it has been almost taken for granted that we should digitise museums because the future is digital and because people want experiences. But then you forget what is unique when people meet art. We must ask ourselves: Is that really the future, or is it just our opinion that it is? What is the right attitude here? We are part of that development, and it does benefit us a lot when people e.g. share our works on social media, since it is free adver-

I find it beautiful that people come here perhaps mainly to be entertained but may leave with a very different attitude and a very different understanding than they came with. A museum has to be a place where people actively take part and don't just passively receive.

tisement. However, I usually describe ARoS as first and foremost a mental fitness centre. Just as in a real fitness centre, it makes no sense over a lengthy period to just lift the same weights or run at the same pace. Some development is required. It requires an effort to move from one level to the next, and that is also how it should be at an art museum. It must help you move from one level to the next as a human being. We don't do that just by pleasing the crowds. Newspapers made a huge mistake when they started running after the audience; when they forgot that they were an authority. Museums could make the same mistake. The greatest potential mistake, however, is when museums believe they are more for the past than for the future."

And now, we are back at being an alternative to filter bubbles ... Is that in fact the role of the art museum in the future?

"In a manner of speaking, yes. If I make a survey and ask you what kind of art you would like, you will most likely answer based on your own experience – what you have seen before. You may not necessarily know what you would like. We know more about contemporary art in this place than most people do. I may know of an artist who really could move you and your view of life."

This, then, is where authority comes into the picture?

"Authority, yes, but also the belief that we may mean something for our society. For me, the most important discussion is what the purpose of art is and what our justification is. I am occupied by building an institution that also can contribute to change; not just in relation to how we look at art, but also in relation to how we act as people in our society."

THE DUAL GAZE

You have in fact been very successful in drawing people to your museum. How do you maintain the balance between giving people what they want and what you as a professional or an authority think they need?

"That is a delicate balance. After all, I am measured according to whether the museum is being used and if people come in through the door. My way of thinking is that when people buy a ticket or something in the café, they help crowdfund our next project. However, we don't run a museum to make money; we make money to become a better museum, to quote a good colleague. But I would like to have more people visit AroS. If we get 600,000 or 700,000 people through the house in a year, that is also a signal to the politicians that people in fact want museums. Blockbusters pull people in, but if we only focus on those, we will eventually reduce ourselves to being a trend, and trends die. On the other hand, if we only focus on our integrity and art professionalism, we risk that our exhibitions become irrelevant, and then we will cheat the audience of the experience they may get through art. Hence, it is a matter of having an eye for both needs. I would like people to show up because we tell relevant stories in a good way."

ENLIGHTENMENT VS. ENTERTAINMENT

Do you see yourself as part of something that offers entertainment or enlightenment?

"I am part of something that offers enlightenment, and that motivates me. Still, I also know that ARoS is entertainment to many people. I find it beautiful that people come here perhaps mainly to be entertained but may leave with a very different attitude and a very »

SCENARIO
MAGAZINE

Copenhagen Institute for Futures Studies

ANALYSES TRENDS IDEAS FUTURES

> It is almost impossible to become part of that league, but it is a good challenge – and if we realise it, we may have a situation where the art comes in first place precisely because we have created the economy for it.

different understanding than they came with. A museum has to be a place where people actively take part and don't just passively receive. Hence, for me, it isn't just a matter of pushing buttons to make more people come through the door, but also of how we contribute to democratic society."

Erlend Høyersten has grand plans for ARoS' future, among other things based on an idea he got five years ago. Today, this implies an ambitious underground extension designed by light and installation artist James Turrell in collaboration with architects Schmidt Hammer Lassen, who also designed the original ARoS. The extension will house a gigantic piece of art by Turrell called The Dome, and a new, large gallery, connected by corridors that in themselves will be an experience.

Above ground between the dome and the current museum there will be a space for an annual architecture pavilion. The project is on the drawing board and is now entering the final phase of financing. I ask Høyersten why the already rather sizeable museum needs to be expanded.

"It is part of my strategy to open the museum more and more, but also to attract more people and have room for them all. When I started, there was an almost entire floor of the museum that was closed to the public, which is now open. In ARoS Public, as we call it, we have studios, conversation salons, and an artist residency distributed among 1,900 square metres. We already have quite a lot of visitors, but not room enough. ARoS is only built to accept 200,000 visitors a year, but we are currently at three or four times that capacity. It is also a matter of creating a more sustainable economy in the long run."

Yet doesn't it usually go the other way? The Royal Theatre in Copenhagen e.g. has too many buildings and large operating costs, and some critics say this takes money away from the art itself…

"I see exactly the opposite – as a means for communicating art well and being able to afford taking chances in the future, it is a matter of making something with high attractiveness. James Turrell is by some described as the Michelangelo of our time, and he will be a huge attraction, making us able to get more travelling visitors. We already have a good grip on the regional audience, but if we want to grow and do the things we want to do, we also need to attract e.g. more Germans, Swedes, and Norwegians who don't travel just for the art, but also for the architecture. When I came to ARoS, I started working with that level of ambition and said that we should strive to be among the 20 most important art museums in the world. It is almost impossible to become part of that league, but it is a good challenge – and if we realise it, we may have a situation where the art comes in first place precisely because we have created the economy for it."

What about your own future? What do you dream of?

"Well … I never planned my career. And I am happy where I am now. Yet, in some way it is probably tied to whether we find the money for the extension, which is what I dream of. That creates a perspective, but also a timeframe for me. I currently work on a three-year contract, but if the extension becomes a reality, it might be extended. If it doesn't become a reality, I will need to consider the future of ARoS in another light, and with that, also my own scenario. Perhaps it will engage me, or perhaps it will demotivate me. Time will tell."

Our time with Erlend Høyersten is almost up, and soon, the museum will be full of guests for the opening.

"Want to play a game?" he asks when we return to the area outside the exhibition proper, where the ping-pong tables are set up. Soon, the four of us have bats in our hands, and in this somewhat surprising way, we end an interview about art and future with a game of around-the-table. Relational aesthetical   «

CHAPLIN 13e

FILMREIFE WEIHNACHTEN MIT DEN CHAPLINS!

IM MANOIR DE BAN UND IM PARK, CORSIER SUR VEVEY AM GENFER SEE, SCHWEIZ

Weihnachten voller Magie und Zauber am Ende des Gedenkjahres zum 130. Geburtstag von Charlie Chaplin. Filmvorführungen, Lichtspiele und traumhafte Atmosphären werden die ganze Familie verzaubern, sowohl im Inneren des Manoir de Ban wie auch im Park.
Ort: Manoir de Ban und im Park, Chaplin's World Corsier sur Vevey am Genfer See, Schweiz

Chaplin's World TM © Bubbles Incorporated

Chaplin's WORLD

www.ingramcontent.com/pod-product-compliance
Lightning Source LLC
Chambersburg PA
CBHW040413220526
45473CB00004B/1230